THE WITCH-CRAFTING HANDBOOK

MAGICAL PROJECTS AND RECIPES FOR YOU AND YOUR HOME

HELENA GARCIA

Photography by Patricia Niven
Illustrations by Andrea Kett

Hardie Grant
QUADRILLE

To my grandmother, the original Flora -
thank you for your love and dedication.

And to my daughter Flora,
my little witch in training.

Cooking note: The recipes in this book were tested
in a fan-assisted [convection] oven. If your oven is
not fan-assisted, raise the Celsius temperatures given
throughout by 20°C.

The Fahrenheit temperatures in the book are for
regular (non-fan) ovens.

CONTENTS

INTRODUCTION ⌒⌒

Witches - aren't they the most fascinating creatures? Whether real or not, witches have always been and still remain a mystery full of ambiguity.

As a child I always chose to play the role of the witch, the villain of the story ... the most fun character in the play. When I looked into the role of witches, I often felt they were misunderstood. Why were they so feared, I wondered? They seemed like self-sufficient people, deeply connected to nature, knowledgeable and creative – yet if you crossed them, they would make you suffer. Well, I sure could relate to that.

Looking back now, I can see that my paternal grandmother had such a significant influence on my upbringing. She would have been described as a 'kitchen witch' if that had been a recognised term back then – being inventive in the kitchen, using a combination of home-grown and foraged ingredients, not just for cooking but for other purposes like cleaning, medicine, cosmetics. And keeping an array of furry friends. All I aspired to in life!

Now, I find myself drawn back to the passions of my childhood and eager to share them with those of you who, like me, favoured an afternoon picking twigs and turning them into magic wands.

This witch-crafting handbook is a pretty accurate representation of everything I love to make. I truly believe that those who are crafty in the kitchen can transfer their creative skills to other areas. Fashion and interiors have been a life-long passion for me; the kitchen, however, remains the most important room in the house. It's where true magic is made – and make no mistake, transforming simple ingredients into a wholesome meal is a love enchantment.

I use the term 'witch-crafting' to refer to the art of making your own spooky fashion accessories, home decorations, potions and concoctions. Connecting history and folklore to the items we craft gives them a deeper meaning. When possible, introducing a touch of nature also adds significance.

I invite and encourage you to look deeper into tradition; more often than not, simple practices of everyday life will have their roots in some sort of fear of witches or the devil. It's absurd and fascinating in equal measure, yet ancient practices are not to be dismissed, as there's wisdom to be rediscovered.

My main objective, however, will always be to inspire and tempt you to the 'dark' side. It is simply more fun! As the old saying goes: go to Heaven for the climate and Hell for the company.

OLD WITCH TALES AND REMEDIES

There's a lot to be learned from ancient knowledge of medicinal plants, remedies and concoctions. I once read that a thousand-year-old recipe for an eye salve found in an old Anglo-Saxon medical manuscript killed MRSA, when tested in a laboratory, faster than any modern antibiotic. The recipe called for onion, garlic, wine and cow's bile to be mashed together and kept in a bronze vessel for nine days and nine nights. Compared to modern medicine this probably sounds like Hocus Pocus, but to me it sounds like something my grandmother would swear by.

My siblings and I spent the summer holidays during our school years with our grandmother in northern Spain. Her house, an old village cottage with exposed beams and wrought-iron stoves, has been in the family for generations and it is very much unchanged from when it was first built in the early 1800s. She grew her own vegetables and kept pigs and chickens. I still remember being sent to the local farm with a metal churn to pick up milk from cows that had just been milked that very morning. Then she would boil it to pasteurise it. I long for those simpler days. Bike rides, mushroom picking and preparing hearty meals with her in the kitchen … once, though, hundreds of ants walked into the pot and she let us eat the stew like nothing had happened. We thought they were little burnt bits; she thought it was added protein.

  My love of cooking and old-fashioned homemaking can easily be traced back to her. She made all her own clothes and the clothes for her children, and she embroidered, crocheted and had homemade beauty treatments, recipes and useful household suggestions – some that definitely worked and others that were slightly more dubious. This little section of the book is based on her tales and the tales of other resourceful wise witches.

As a remedy for a burn, use the slime of a snail
As disgusting as it sounds, this method has been proven by modern science to be efficient. On the other hand, aloe vera or a slice of raw potato work perfectly well to soothe small burns, so I'll stick with the plant-based remedy.

A cure for falling hair
The stinging nettle is such a common yet magical plant. Not only do the leaves provide a variety of nutrients, the root controls DHT levels, which are linked to hair loss or growth. It was known in the

Middle Ages as a cure for baldness and it seems our ancestors were on to something here.

In a bowl, infuse 90g [1 cup minus 2 tsp] of young nettle leaves (pick the ones from the top 10cm [4in] of the plant) in 90ml [6 Tbsp] of warm cider vinegar. Steep for 30 minutes. Gently massage the infusion into your scalp every day for 5 minutes.

Thyme tea to relieve a cough

Thyme is one of my favourite culinary herbs, for both savoury and sweet treats. You may remember my Sandworm Lemon and Thyme Cupcakes from *The Wicked Baker*. Thyme, however, has other beneficial properties. It helps against bacterial infections and acts as a natural expectorant, relaxing the respiratory tract and helping to get rid of mucus.

Make 1 cup of thyme tea by steeping 3 fresh thyme sprigs (or 1 Tbsp dried thyme) in 1 cup of boiling water. Add sugar or honey to taste, and drink.

Natural air freshener and purifier

In a sterilised container, add 100g [3½oz] fresh eucalyptus leaves to 750ml [3¼ cups] white wine vinegar. Leave to infuse for 2 weeks. Strain the liquid through a muslin cloth [cheesecloth] into an open container and leave in a room to freshen the air.

To remove a wart

OK, this one is rather dubious, but there may be some witches willing to try anything, so I've included it anyway.

In order to remove a wart, rub it with fresh sloe juice every day until it disappears. Sloes are fairly common in the UK, and best picked after the first frost.

Make candles last longer

Witches are renowned for burning plenty of candles, so to make them last longer, place them in the freezer for a few hours before use.

Bad smell remedies

Prevent stinking out the cottage by adding a little lemon juice to the cauldron when cooking cabbages.

When painting the walls, cut an onion in half and place each half, cut-side up, in opposite corners of the room.

After cooking smelly ingredients like eye of newt or toe of frog in a standard saucepan, sometimes the smell lingers in the pan. Simply add 1 tsp mustard powder to the washing-up liquid when you clean it, and the smells disappear like magic. Alternatively, you can boil a little vinegar in the pan for a minute or so before cleaning as normal.

Pesky stains

Rub table salt inside teacups to remove stains after a witches' tea party.

To remove a stain from a saucepan, cook rhubarb or apple in it and witness the stains disappear.

Open fires in the cottage can cause a spark of wood or coal to burn the carpet. To remove the burn stain, rub the area well with the cut side of an onion.

Clean the windows with either a little vinegar diluted in warm water, or use slightly damp newspaper crumpled into a ball, then dry it with dry newspaper.

Clean grime formed between tiles with a paste made from bicarbonate of soda [baking soda] mixed with bleach. I like to use my husband's toothbrush to rub the paste (cackle, cackle).

Beauty tips for witches

Mix 1 Tbsp bicarbonate of soda [baking soda] in a cup of warm water for a few minutes, then soak your fingertips in it. Dry with a clean cloth and apply almond oil to the cuticles. This will strengthen your nails.

For thicker eyelashes and eyebrows, apply castor oil to them using a thin brush (something like a lipstick brush). This totally works and I do it regularly.

To maintain lovely smooth feet and prevent cracked skin, warm a little olive oil in the cauldron and massage your whole foot with it once a week.

After flying all night, your eyes will look tired and dark circles will form. Put some cotton wool pads in a jar and cover them with witch hazel. Store in the fridge and apply when you need to.

Formula for shiny hair

Below is a remedy to rescue dull-looking hair, although a simpler way to give it shine is to massage a beaten egg yolk into your hair every week in between rinses.

INGREDIENTS
140ml [1 cup] rum
2 lavender sprigs
marrow of 1 beef bone
a few drops cider vinegar

Warm the rum in a saucepan over a low heat until simmering, then remove from the heat and add the lavender sprigs. Leave to infuse for 1 hour.

Melt the marrow from the beef bone in a heatproof bowl set over a pan of gently simmering water, making sure the base of the bowl isn't touching the water. Mix in the lavender-infused rum and heat gently until warm.

Gently massage the mixture onto your scalp, then wrap your hair in a towel. Leave for 1 hour, then shampoo once to get rid of the mixture. Add a few drops of cider vinegar to your hair and shampoo again. Repeat twice a month.

Finally, a homemade shampoo formula for your trusted wolf familiar (or any other canine): in a bottle or other container, mix 1 part apple cider vinegar and 2 parts delicate handwash detergent with 3 parts water. I sometimes add a little aloe vera gel too.

WITCH FACTS AND INTERESTING ACTS

It is fascinating to learn that many of our peculiar superstitious acts were born out of fear of witches, devils and ghosts. Below I have summarised a few interesting facts and some witch-related behaviours that still take place in modern society.

In the Middle Ages it was believed that mistletoe had the magical ability to stop an epileptic episode as well as keeping witches at bay. Nowadays we hang it above the door and remove a berry with each kiss received.

The act of throwing salt over our left shoulder is yet another example of an ancient superstition that is still practised today.

This act goes back as far as 3,500 BC and it reflects the prized possession salt once was. After all, the word 'salary' is derived from salt.

Our ancestors used to cut a cross at the base of cabbages, Brussels sprouts and lettuces to ward off evil spirits who hid between their leaves. If you ingested these foods uncut, you ran the risk of getting a stomach upset or suffering from some sort of illness. We keep being told by chefs to cut that little cross to help the vegetables cook evenly, but trust me, they will cook regardless. Without knowing it, we are victims of a medieval superstitious belief.

In the 18th and 19th centuries, it was the custom to hang witches' balls on the windows or doors to ward off witches and evil spirits. Witches' balls are reflective mirrored glass, silver, red or green balls, usually believed to entrap witches when they look at their own reflection. They are still around. You often find them in antique shops and in auctions. They look like Christmas baubles, just slightly bigger.

Although the fear of the number 13 pre-dates Christianity, it is often attributed to the last supper, where Judas, the 13th guest at the table, betrayed Jesus who was then crucified on a Friday – hence the suspicion around Friday 13th. Consequently, in the 1600s, if you were in a group of 13 people, you might be accused of being a witch.

Mince pies date back to medieval times, but their original form would look unrecognisable today. They were rectangular in shape and the pastry shells were known as 'coffins' – a great piece of trivia for us goths. The coffin was a mere vessel in which to cook the real meal. They were larger pies meant to be shared. These 'coffins' were probably thrown away after cooking, although I'm sure poorer families would have eaten them. The filling was savoury; a 1591 recipe for mince pie lists mutton or beef as its main ingredient, combined with suet, cloves and dried fruits.

Midsummer spells

Of the many bizarre and spooky witchy tales I've read, the onion spell one must be up there. The night before the winter solstice on 20 December was once known as St Thomas's Eve. On this night, it was believed that St Thomas rode around the streets at midnight in a fiery chariot, and all the dead men christened with the name of Thomas rose from their graves and joined him as he led them towards the church, where he prayed and then disappeared.

The dead Thomases then went back to their underground beds. On this night, young maidens wishing to see a vision of their true love would peel a red onion (a St Thomas onion) and stick nine pins into it, eight forming a circle around it and one right on top. They would then recite:

> Good Saint Thomas, do me right
> Send me true love this night,
> In his clothes and his array,
> which he weareth every day.

They would then place the onion under their pillow to dream of their future husband. The following night, 21 December, was believed to be a night when spirits walked around, and although it was dangerous to be outdoors, it was considered a prosperous night full of magic.

The act of making a wish when blowing out birthday candles also has a peculiar witchy past. The ancient Greeks used to bake round cakes with candles on top in worship of the moon goddess Artemis. The cake represented the moon and the burning candles the moonlight. Later on, Christian religions used the candle to represent eternal life.

Candle magic is still practised as a simple form of wish casting. To cast a candle spell, always use new candles, as old ones may be charged with negative energy. Different colours reflect different wishes. Use white for cleansing, purity and new beginnings, gold for good fortune and money, silver and yellow for reflection, purple to get rid of negativity, green for vitality, fertility and healing, brown for protection, red for love, orange for attraction, pink for friendship, blue for its calming purpose and black to repel anything.

In rural Britain, many people believed elder trees were witches and kept them well away from their homes. On the other hand, the rowan tree was believed to have protective properties and was often planted near houses. Incidentally, I have both an elder and a rowan tree in my garden.

According to the Native American Newuk tribe, when a virtuous person died, she would become a great horned owl. If she were wicked, she would turn into a barn owl.

THE WITCH'S WARDROBE

METALLIC BESOMS ～⌒

MAKES 3

MATERIALS
3 wooden sticks (look for
  ones with imperfections
  and twists and turns)
bunch of dried wheat stalks
string or tape
white spray paint
silver metallic spray paint
a selection of artificial leaves
  on wire
copper metallic spray paint
artificial seed pods
wired ribbon bow
rose gold metallic spray paint

EQUIPMENT
sponge
electric saw (optional)
glue gun

If you think a witch's favourite method of transport
is a simple tree branch with attached bristles, think
again - because we are going to pimp this ride.
There are endless possibilities when it comes to
decorating your broom. Flowers, feathers, ribbons,
etc. can be added all around. The bristles don't
need to be made of natural straw, either: you can
use other materials. In this tutorial I'm going for a
high-end fashion take on the old broomstick, using
a metallic finish and a selection of unusual materials
for the bristles.

Start by going on a long woodland walk in search of
unusual-looking tree branches that would work well
as a stick for the brooms. Store them indoors for about
a week until they are fully dry. Clean them well with
a damp sponge, peeling away any loose bark, then cut
them to the desired length – I used an electric saw.
   To make the wheat besom, arrange the dried wheat
stalks next to each other in a single layer on a long
table. Place your stick in the middle and gather the
wheat stalks around it, holding them together with
your hands. Tie some string (or tape) around the top
and wrap the string around a couple of times, securing
it together at the end. Repeat this process twice more,
spacing the bindings an equal distance apart. Trim the
tops so they're uniform.
   Spray the whole thing with the white spray paint and
leave until fully dry. Once dry, spray again with silver,
and let it dry completely.
   For the copper besom, gather your artificial leaves
and attach them with string or tape to the wooden stick
as before. Once they're secure, spread them outwards
so they fan out. Give the besom a white base coat, then
spray in copper and leave until fully dry.
   Finally, to make the rose gold besom, repeat the
previous process using the artificial seed pods for
bristles and attaching a wired ribbon bow as a
decoration using a glue gun. Spray paint it white,
then add the rose gold coat. Leave until fully dry.

GHOST IN FLORAL SHEETS PENDANT

MAKES 1

MATERIALS
foil
ivory Fimo clay
mini screw eyelets
acrylic paints
varnish
your choice of necklace
ribbon (optional)

EQUIPMENT
straw
paintbrushes

I have a weakness for cute ghosts in general, floral ghosts in particular. The lovely Priya from my *Bake Off* class of 2019 always laughs at the fact I added buttercream flowers to my ghost cake on one of the challenges. The truth is that I love adding feminine touches to spooky concepts. This ghost pendant is the result of a little sketch I did for a print design. Using clay means anyone can make their own: you could even imitate your own floral sheets when painting it.

Start by moulding the general ghost shape out of foil. My ghost was 3cm [1¼in] tall. This will be what creates a hollow centre. If we were to make the ghost from a solid clump of clay, it would probably crack when baking.
   Roll out a piece of clay into a circle big enough to wrap around the foil. Drape it over the foil and make some folds with your fingers to imitate fabric creases.
   Cut out the holes for the eyes and mouth using the straw. Stick the mini screw eyelets to the top of the head – these will be used to attach it to the necklace – then bake according to the manufacturer's instructions.
   Remove from the oven and leave to cool, then paint it with a floral design. I opted for roses, but you can paint anything you like.
   Finally, give it a coat or two of varnish, then thread the necklace through the eyelets, or thread a ribbon through the eyelets and tie it onto the chain.

AMANITA MUSCARIA CHILD'S HAT

MATERIALS
cardboard
0.5m [½yd] cotton muslin
   or any sheer white fabric,
   for the gills
0.5m [½yd] red velvet fabric,
   for the cap
artificial flowers, for the white
   spots
cotton ribbon
wadding or batting
pillow stuffing

EQUIPMENT
scissors
stapler
Stanley knife
glue gun
masking tape

I could write a whole chapter dedicated to this iconic mushroom. To give you a little insight into the folklore of the fly agaric, witches were believed to use it to get high and 'fly'. In order to avoid the vomit-inducing effects of consuming it, they used to make it into an ointment, which they then rubbed on the ends of their broomsticks before inserting them into their vaginas or rubbing them underneath their arms.

Siberian tribes fed these mushrooms to their reindeer and then drank their urine, which gave them hallucinations of their reindeer flying through space (hence the story of reindeer flying at Christmas, and the possible origin of Santa Claus's red and white suit).

The hat is perfect for a child's costume, but it could be made in any size. There's no need for a sewing machine, either, as everything is glued on.

Start by measuring the circumference of the child's head. Cut a 4cm [1½in] wide strip of cardboard to a length 1.5cm [⅝in] longer than the head circumference and staple the ends together. Place on your child's head and use another 2 strips of cardboard of the same width to reach from the front to the back of the head and from one side to the other to form a cross. Remove from the child's head and secure with the stapler. This will form the cap.

To make the brim of the hat, draw a circle on a piece of cardboard with your desired diameter. For my 2½-year-old with a head circumference of 48cm [19in], I drew a circle with a diameter of 36cm [14in]. Cut it out using scissors or the Stanley knife.

Place the cap we made in the first step in the middle of the cardboard circle and draw around it. It should be oval, like the shape of the head. Cut this shape out with the Stanley knife. You should now have a

cont …

doughnut shape, with a hole in the middle. This is the brim.

Attach the cap to the brim using the glue gun on the base and sides.

Cut another 4 cardboard strips like the ones used on the cap – 4cm [1½in] wide and long enough to go across the entire hat. Bend the ends and glue them at the base.

To make the gills, cut out a circle from the white fabric with a diameter 30cm [12in] larger than the cardboard one (in my case, the cardboard brim was 36cm [14in], so the fabric brim was 66cm [26in] in diameter). And for the inner oval, cut out an oval 20cm [8in] larger than the cardboard one.

Turn your cardboard hat upside down and start gathering the inner circle of the fabric brim into the oval hole of the cardboard hat using the glue gun. You want to overlap bits of fabric with glue to create creases.

Pull your fabric towards the outer side of the brim, gather it like before and glue in place.

Cut a circle out of the red velvet fabric that is 10cm [4in] larger in circumference than the cardboard brim. Place the wadding or batting on top, then cut out a circle from it around 5cm [2in] smaller than the velvet.

Centre the wadding on top of the cardboard hat frame and glue it in place, stretching it around and gluing it to cover the whole cap. Trim the edges if necessary.

Turn the hat upside down and fill it with the pillow stuffing through the holes.

Cut 2 pieces of cotton ribbon and glue them at each side of the inner circle.

Turn it the right way up and attach the red velvet circle, starting at the top, gluing it with the glue gun and continuing all the way to the edge. Trim the excess fabric. Glue on the white artificial flowers to imitate the white spots, some individual ones and some in clusters.

Now the hardest step is getting your child to put the hat on. Good luck!

CAT POM-POM BRACELET ⌒◎

MAKES 1

MATERIALS
0.5m [½yd] black faux fur
  fabric
stuffing
nose and whiskers (optional –
  look for soft toy supplies)
black felt
18cm [7in] length of red
  ribbon (optional)
PU leather wrist strap
  (colour of your choice)

EQUIPMENT
glue gun
scissors
needle and thread

In my last crafting book, I made some old Hollywood-style cat pom-pom slippers to represent a witch's infamous familiar. This time around I thought we could translate that idea into a bracelet. Who hasn't made pom-poms with a couple of rings made out of cardboard and some knitting wool? That's one option. The other option is to make the pom-pom out of faux fur, which is what I've chosen to do here. I originally gave the cat pom-pom eyes, but it looked way too cute. Adding just the ears, nose and whiskers makes it obvious what animal it is without giving it a toy-like look.

Start by making the pom-pom. Draw a circle on the flat surface of the faux fur fabric. The diameter should reflect the size you would like your pom-pom cat to be.

Cut out the circle, avoiding cutting the fur as much as possible: try to just cut the fabric the fur is attached to.

Stitch all around the circle in order to gather the fabric into a ball. Pull the thread and start gathering the fabric together, then fill it with the stuffing and continue to gather it until it closes. Sew it shut.

Move the fur around to create space for the nose and whiskers and glue into place.

Cut ears out of the black felt and glue them on. If you want a bow, tie the red ribbon into a bow and stick onto the base of one of the cat's ears with the glue gun.

To attach the cat to the bracelet strap, push the fur aside around the base and glue it flat. Cut out a rectangular piece of felt and secure it from the inside of the bracelet upwards with the glue gun. Glue the base of the pom-pom to the felt so the bracelet strap is wedged between the pom-pom and the felt.

WITCHY BAKER'S HAT ~

MAKES 1

MATERIALS
1.4m [1½yd] buckram (you can also use craft foam or cardboard) for the hat frame
1.4m [1½yd] 12-gauge wire
1.8m [2yd] white cotton fabric
white thread

EQUIPMENT
scissors
sewing machine (for buckram frame option)
hand sewing needle
glue gun
curved upholstery needle

As October drew closer the year I took part in *The Great British Bake Off*, panic set in as I hadn't come up with my Halloween costume for that year. I follow this little tradition of dressing as a witch every Halloween. I'm not talking black gowns and pointy hats here (although I love the traditional witch look) - I like to give my witch costume a different theme each year. There was no other choice that year than dressing as a baker, so I quickly took pen and paper and drew the basics - a giant whisk 'broomstick', a Victorian apron and a chef's hat with a cone. I went to my hardware store and bought some pipes and cables to make the whisk, but when it came to the hat, more expert hands were needed. My friend Chelsey's mum, Julane, who runs a costume wonderland in Illinois stepped in and made the baker's hat of my dreams. When she saw the picture, she questioned the size. 'Are you sure you want it that big?' she asked. 'Yes, Julane,' I said, 'go for it!' And so she did - and what's more, she has shared the instructions so you too can crown yourself a Kitchen Witch extraordinaire.

Measure the circumference of the wearer's head and calculate the diameter.

Create the framework for the witchy baker hat. For the hat band, cut out a rectangular section of your frame material measuring 12.5cm [5in] in height and 2.5cm [1in] more in width than the circumference measurement. For the brim, cut a circle of the frame material 48cm [19in] in diameter. In the centre, cut a circle 2.5cm [1in] less than the diameter of the head size. Form the wire into a circle that will fit around the outer edge of the brim. If using buckram, zigzag stitch the wire to the edge of the buckram to stabilize the brim of the hat. If using craft foam, use your glue gun to secure the wire. This will give support to the weight

cont ...

of the hat. Form the witchy hat cone by cutting a conical (triangular) section of the frame material 40cm [16in] in height with the point at the top and the width 2.5cm [1in] from the bottom to match that of the head circumference. Join the sides together by hand stitching or using hot glue, overlapping to create a tight point and a conical shape.

Create the cotton pattern pieces to cover the framework. White cotton is the traditional colour and fabric of a baker's hat, but feel free to use a colour or pattern to suit your personality. Using the frame pieces as your pattern, first cut a piece of white cotton the same size as the cone section. To cover the top of the brim, cut a piece of fabric to the size of the diameter of the brim plus a 1.5cm [⅝in] seam allowance. For the puffy baker hat section, cut a rectangle of white fabric measuring 150 x 23cm [59 x 9in]. Cut another section of white fabric to the width of the hat band, with 1.5cm [⅝in] seam allowances on each side.

Assembling fun!

Wrap the cotton cone cover around the cone frame and sew the two sides together at the back, or wrap the fabric around the cone, tucking the fabric under for a clean finish, and secure with the glue gun.

The top and bottom of your puffy baker hat cotton section is 150cm [59in]. Hand-sew or run machine gather stitches along the bottom edge. Do not pull the gathers together yet! Sew the top of the puffy baker hat section to the top of the outer edge of the cotton witch brim section, with the right-side facing down, leaving a 1.5cm [⅝in] seam allowance at the start of your seam.

Take the cotton witch brim pattern piece and sew the outer circle edge to the top of the puffy baker hat section. Once you have sewn this together, stitch down the side seam of the puffy baker hat section where the ends have met. Turn right side out. Fit this over the top side of the brim. You can secure it in place either by sewing around the top outer edge of the brim (not catching the puffy baker hat section) with your machine, or by hand tacking into place in at least five evenly spaced places. (If using craft foam or cardboard, you can attach with glue in a few places.)

At the centre circle of the brim, glue the edge of the cotton fabric to the frame. Cut small slits every 2cm [¾in] so you can turn down the excess to achieve a clean look on the outside, while providing an inner stem to which you can secure the puffy baker hat band.

Slip the cotton witch peak into the open centre circle of the brim until it fits snugly. Secure to the stem of the centre brim circle with a few hand stitches or stick in place with glue. Trim any excess from the peak section inside below the brim.

Sew the ends of the cotton hat band together. Pull the gathers from the cotton puffy baker hat section until they evenly fit across the top edge of the cotton hat band. Sew those pieces together so the seam is on the inside. Secure that to the band frame 5cm [2in] from the bottom on the outside of the band, with the seam going to the top. This can be done either by sewing machine, hand sewing or using your glue gun.

Turn the fabric from the cotton band section down and under into the band frame. Secure with stitches or glue to the inside of the band.

The final step is to secure the band to the turned down stem section of the witch hat where the brim meets the peak. The band should fit on the outside of the turned down stem by pushing it as far up as you can and securing tightly with glue or stitches. This is the most difficult part of the project as you are working inside the hat. A curved upholstery needle will come in handy if you choose to stitch this part together.

Voilà! Wear your witchy baker hat while you make your spooky concoctions!

EVIL EYE CHOKER ~◞

MAKES 1

MATERIALS
5cm [2½in] square piece of
  black felt
1 crystal button
1 x 14mm oval-shaped red
  sew-on rhinestone
1 x 7mm pearl bead
2 x 6mm pearl beads
4 x 4mm pearl beads
16 x 3mm pearl beads
1m [1yd] black velvet ribbon
  [2.5cm/1in wide]
1m [1yd] black gathered
  organza trim
2 x 38mm ribbon end clamps
split rings
chain
lobster clasp
glass evil eye charm
11mm teardrop bead
jewellery pin

EQUIPMENT
needle and thread
scissors
flat-nose jewellery pliers

It is said the eyes are the gateway into the soul. The eye of Horus and the eye of Providence represent wisdom, protection, omniscience and truth, among other things. In the past few years, the Evil Eye, an amulet which is meant to ward off evil, has been widely used in the world of fashion. Prints, bracelets and pendants are all adorned with this ancient symbol. In this project, we insert the handmade eye amulet into a velvet choker with an adjustable chain closure.

To make the eye, draw an eye shape on the felt, about 5cm [2in] wide by 3.5cm [1¼in] high. Sew the crystal button (I found one with a crystal in the middle and rhinestones around it) into the centre. This will be the pupil and iris.

Sew the red oval bead to the corner of the eye shape. This will be the lacrimal gland, where the tears drop from. Next, sew the 7mm pearl in the middle, above the pupil, with one 6mm pearl on either side. Follow up with 2 x 4mm pearls on either side, then continue to sew around the rest of the eye shape with the 3mm pearls.

Use the velvet ribbon to measure around your neck and cut 2 pieces, each about 4cm [1½in] shorter than your neck.

Pin the organza trim along the top and bottom of one piece of ribbon and sew it on, leaving 6.5mm [¼in] plain ribbon at each end for the ribbon end clamp. Sew the eye into the middle of the ribbon, then pin and attach the second piece of velvet ribbon to the back, with the fluffy side out.

Finally, attach the clamps with the flat-nose pliers, then attach the chain and lobster clasp. Attach the little evil eye charm to the end of the chain with the teardrop bead hanging off it using a jewellery pin and looping the charm at both ends. On one end, add the teardrop bead; loop the other end around the chain.

ALL-SEEING EYE GLOVES

MAKES 1 PAIR

MATERIALS
10cm [4in] square piece black
  felt
2 black 5mm beads for pupils
handful of blue 2mm beads
handful of 7mm rectangular
  blue sew-on rhinestones
2 x 8mm oval-shaped red
  sew-on rhinestones
handful of small tube-shaped
  silver beads
handful of 0.5mm clear sew-
  on rhinestones
handful of 0.4mm clear sew-
  on rhinestones
pair of black velvet or gold
  lurex gloves (vintage ones
  are easier to find)
10 x 14mm oval-shaped red
  sew-on rhinestones, for the
  nails
10 x 15mm oval-shaped red
  sew-on rhinestones

EQUIPMENT
scissors
needle and thread

I thought it would be nice to complement the choker on page 27 with these gloves. I've seen eye appliqués similar to these online, so I thought I'd give you the instructions to make your own. It's not actually too complicated, but if you haven't got the patience or time, simply buy something similar and sew it on. Attaching nails to the end of the glove fingers is of course, one of the staple ideas of surrealist designer Elsa Schiaparelli. I have a few gloves with long nails on them, but this is the first time I have used rhinestones. I think they work great.

To make the eyes, draw an eye shape on the felt, about 4cm [1½in] wide by 3cm [1¼in] high. Cut it out and use it as a template to cut a second one.

Sew the black bead in the middle. This will be the pupil. Now sew the little blue 2mm spacer beads around the pupil bead in 2 circles to form the iris. Add a ring of the blue rectangular rhinestone beads around them.

Sew the 8mm oval-shaped red bead to the left corner of the eye. This will be the lacrimal gland, where the tears drop from. Then sew the small silver tube beads around the oval shape of the eye.

Finish the outside of the eye with the clear rhinestones, sewing 4 x 0.5mm ones at the top and bottom centre of the eye and completing the rest of the shape with the 0.4mm rhinestones, leaving a space for 1 x 15mm oval-shaped red rhinestone, which will act as a teardrop.

Set the eye appliqués aside and start sewing the nails onto the fingertips of the gloves. I actually put my hands into the gloves to do this and didn't have any accidents.

After all the nails are in place, sew the eye appliqués into the centre of the top of each glove. Add the rest of the 15mm oval-shaped red rhinestones, 1 as an extra teardrop and 3 as cyelashes.

BEADED SPIDER KNEE-HIGH SOCKS

MAKES 1 PAIR

MATERIALS
2 x 6mm pearls
2 x 8mm pearls
2 flat-head jewellery pins
  (silver or gold plated,
  depending on your chosen
  colours)
0.5mm copper wire
tube beads
4mm Swarovski beads
crystal spiderwebs or similar
selection of sequins, sequin
  flowers and beads in your
  chosen colour scheme

EQUIPMENT
jewellery pliers
needle and thread

I adore these socks. The beaded spiders are subtle, but they definitely make their mark. Once you learn how to make them, you can use them as brooches, pendants, on headbands or as Christmas ornaments. The colour combinations on this project are endless: I've opted for silvers and greys, but blacks and golds would look great too. The crystal spiderwebs were from a haberdashery and came with hanging spiders that I removed. If you can't find something similar it doesn't really matter.

Let's make the spiders first. Thread one of the 6mm pearls followed by an 8mm one onto a flat-headed pin, then loop the end with jewellery pliers. This is the spider's body.

Cut 4 pieces of wire, about 5cm [2in] long (you will be cutting them down if necessary). Loop the wire through the spider's body – 2 on either side – and bend them over to create 8 legs.

Plan how you would like the beads to go on the legs, such as tube beads combined with rounded ones for the joints. For these small spiders I've kept them quite simple but when you make a bigger one you can play with a variety of combinations. Always start with the smaller beads nearer the spider's body.

After you fill the legs with beads, twist the ends of the wire into a loop.

To start on the socks, roughly plan where all the sequins and beads will be sewn. Begin around the middle of the shin area in clumps close together, then sew the sequins further away from each other, towards the sides and above and below the central cluster.

I chose to add a crystal spiderweb and beaded spider to each sock. To sew on the beaded spiders, I recommend looping the thread around the middle of the body, between the 2 pearls.

WICKED WITCH HAND BROOCH ～੭

MAKES 1

MATERIALS
hand template (you can draw
it or download mine from
www.witchesbyhelenagarcia.
com/pages/downloads)
A4 piece of 4mm thick black
felt
5 x 10mm red peardrop sew-
on crystal beads (Swarovski
are the best)
3 vintage buttons
3 x 15mm black peardrop
sew-on crystals, for the cuff
3mm emerald Swarovski hot
fix (or glue-on) crystals
4mm emerald Swarovski hot
fix (or glue-on) crystals
6mm emerald Swarovski hot
fix (or glue-on) crystals
brooch pin

EQUIPMENT
sewing scissors
tweezers
crystal glue or hot fix wand
glue gun

Witches being depicted with green skin is a relatively
new concept. Although theories dating back to the
1600s fly about linking the green-faced witch to
torture suffered by the accused women, it is the 1939
film *The Wizard of Oz* that popularised this image.
There is an account from the Spanish pharmacologist
and botanist Andrés Laguna de Segovia in the 1500s
in which he describes a green ointment composed of
nightshade, mandrake, hemlock and henbane being
found in the house of two alleged witches. Either
way, the modern caricature of a wicked witch is that
of a green-skinned hag, and that's the pigment I've
used on this brooch.

Draw or print the hand template on a piece of paper.
Cut it out and pin it on the felt. Using good sewing
scissors, cut the hand shape out of the felt.
   Sew the red peardrop Swarovski crystals onto the
fingertips to look like pointy nails. Sew the vintage
buttons on as rings, to whichever fingers you prefer. If
the buttons stick out too much, it is worth cutting out
the loop to make them flat and gluing them instead.
   Next, sew on the cuff crystals. Once all the large
pieces are in place, it will be much easier to attach
the hot fix ones.
   Start fixing the emerald crystals. It is easier to use
tweezers to hold them in place. Either add a little
glue and hold them down, or stick them in place with
your hot fix wand. Start with the larger ones on the
outer edge.
   Use the smaller crystals around the nail area and
the medium-sized ones to fill in the gaps. Adapt the
size you are using to suit the spaces. Once all crystals
are fixed in place, turn the hand around and glue the
brooch pin to the back using the glue gun.

MOURNING CROWN ∽

MAKES 1

MATERIALS
1 small seashell
gold spray paint
1 x 4cm [1½in] wide velvet
  headband
A4 piece of clear acetate sheet
3 x black beaded appliqués
2 gold pipe cleaners
3–4 black organza flowers
4 small dried flowers with
  stems

EQUIPMENT
scissors
glue gun

This headpiece is somewhat inspired by the Spanish Holy Week (Easter, basically). Rather than pastel eggs and bunny rabbits, we have very dark and macabre-looking processions carrying religious figures to the beat of marching drums. The women wear all black, and lace veils with *peinetas*. It's definitely something to experience.

Start by spray painting the seashell gold. Leave to dry for 2 hours.

Place your headband on the bottom edge of the acetate sheet and use it as a template to draw a 12cm [4½in] curved line. Draw another curved line in an arc reaching about 8.5cm [3⅓in] above this, starting and ending in the same place. This will be your 'halo'. Cut it out.

Use the glue gun to attach the 3 beaded appliqués to the halo, spacing them an equal distance apart. It's best to do the middle one first and then the side ones.

Add a little glue all along the base of the halo and glue it to the middle of the headband about 1cm [½in] from the back to allow space for the decorations that go in front.

To give the acetate more support, cut the pipe cleaners to the width of the acetate halo and glue them along the base, one on top of the other. This will hold the acetate halo in place.

Glue the organza flowers along the front of the headband. You'll need 3 or 4, depending on the size. Cross the dried flowers at the stems and attach them with a little glue to the centre of the halo, on top of the organza flowers. Finally, attach the gold shell.

HOME ACCESSORIES

WITCHES' NIGHT FORAGED ART

MAKES 1

MATERIALS
a selection of autumn leaves,
  twigs, moss, dried flowers,
  grass, bark, etc.
string
paper towels
PVA glue
navy blue A4 card
wire
white acrylic paint

EQUIPMENT
glue gun

Witches' Night, or Walpurgis Night, is celebrated
in northern and central Europe from the evening
of 30 April, concluding on the evening of May Day.
In German folklore, it's believed that on the night
of 30 April, witches would gather at the top of the
Brocken, the highest peak in the Harz mountain
range, and revel with the devil, while the locals built
great bonfires and made a lot of noise to ward off the
evil spirits. I visited the Czech Republic a few years
ago on this date and joined the locals, dressed as a
witch, of course, dancing and screaming around the
bonfire. They brought a 'ceremonial witch' in a cage
carried by a horse and threw her into the fire. It was,
of course, a puppet, but it looked very real ...

First you need to press the flowers and leaves for a few
days between paper towels inside some heavy books.
For the brush bits of the brooms, cut a bunch of long
grass from the garden, tie it with string and hang it up
until it goes brown.

Start with the mountains. Scrunch up some pieces
of paper towel and glue onto the card to create the
mountain shapes, giving them a bit of bulk. Glue on
some moss and paint the tops white to look like snow.

For the house, peel some bark off fire logs or pick it
from the wild from fallen branches. Make sure it is fully
dry. Break it into pieces for the roof and walls. I took
advantage of a natural wood spiral in the bark I used
and cut it into a door shape. Glue on with the glue gun.
For the window, cut a circle out of a yellow leaf. Glue
2 twigs onto it to create the window frame.

For the fire, stick on some pressed yellow leaves and
red acer leaves as flames. Glue twigs underneath for the
fire logs. Brush PVA glue along the base of the picture
and sprinkle over dried leaves and bark for the ground.

For the witches' brooms, attach the dried grass to
twigs using wire. Glue them on with the glue gun.

The moon is made out of a pressed yellow leaf cut
into a circle. Attach dried flowers around the house,
and pine trees made of leaves going up the mountains.

CREATING YOUR WITCH ALTAR

MAKES 1

MATERIALS
dried herbs, flowers and/or
 fruits, for the smudge sticks
string
crystal ball
a selection of books
tarot cards
a selection of fresh or dried
 flowers (I use dried in the
 winter months)
a selection of seasonal foods,
 nuts and berries
candles
cauldron
potion bottles
flash paper (also called
 magician's flash paper)

Creating a space for reflection and spell casting is very personal. The general purpose of an altar is to offer a space of worship, but in my case it is a space of representation and symbolic meaning. I like to display the change of seasons with foliage and/or fruits. Candles and energy crystals are a constant; other items come and go, like the crystal ball, which you can make out of found objects. Get creative and represent your personality; go to the woods and pick foliage, fallen feathers, pine cones and acorns. Choose anything that holds meaning for you.

The first ritual carried out on your altar should be the burning of a smudge stick to cleanse the air, banish negativity and restore balance. Sage is often used for this, but you can add other herbs and flowers (e.g. rosemary, thyme, roses and lavender) or even orange peel studded with cloves. To make it, pick a selection of herbs and flowers, make a bundle, tie it with string and hang it upside down for at least a week until dry.

For your own crystal ball, look for large candlesticks, metal plant holders or vintage decanter bases in antique or charity shops [thrift stores], or even car boot sales [swap meets]. Mine is an old brass kettle stand. The crystal ball itself is not actually that expensive; however, if you are on a budget, use large glass Christmas baubles or a witches' ball if you can find one.

Creating the space is up to you; I like to use a wooden surface with a vintage cloth on top. Stack related books, such as books on palmistry, tasseography (reading tea leaves), tarot reading, magical herbs, crystals, etc.

Make a seasonal flower arrangement; you may also like to add some seasonal foods, nuts and berries.

Decide on your candle colours. In winter, you could use clementines studded with cloves as candle holders.

I firmly believe in the power of intention: write your intention on a piece of flash paper and burn it in the candle flame. It will disappear in your hand. The mere act will keep that intention in your mind, and you will be more likely to fulfill it.

VINTAGE HALLOWEEN HANGERS

MAKES 2

MATERIALS
2 wooden children's hangers
  or a 50cm [20in] square
  piece of walnut wood and
  2 hanger hooks
orange and black paint, or
  colours of your choice
less than 0.5m [½yd] orange
  ribbon
less than 0.5m [½yd] black
  ribbon
vintage images
  (download from www.
  witchesbyhelenagarcia.com/
  pages/downloads or use
  your own)

EQUIPMENT
paper
saw (optional)
sandpaper (optional)
drill (optional)
inkjet Lazertran transfer paper
inkjet printer

This is such an adorable project for your little witch's wardrobe. I've been using vintage decals for craft projects since I was a child. They are great to add to vintage plates to hang on the wall, or to decorate the back of a little wooden chair. You can either buy a vintage Halloween decal online, or, if you are anything like me and have a collection of vintage cards and images saved up, you can get them printed on the right paper. I recommend making the hangers yourself, as then you can play with the design. If you don't have the tools to make them, there are companies out there that will cut the wood for you.

If you are using hangers, remove the metal hooks from the wooden hangers and paint one hanger black and the other orange. Leave to dry completely, then screw the hooks back in.

If you are making the hangers, draw your design on a piece of paper to create a template (mine is 25cm [10in] long and 9cm [3½in] high). Trace the template onto your wood and saw around it carefully. Sand the hanger down and paint it. Drill a little hole for the hook and attach it once the hanger is fully dried.

Print your chosen image onto the transfer paper and cut it out, cutting as close to the edge of the image as possible.

Fill a shallow plate with lukewarm water and submerge the decal. Leave it for 2 minutes, or until the backing paper starts to separate. Peel off the backing paper and transfer the decal onto the centre of the hanger. Smooth out any wrinkles and leave to dry.

Tie the ribbons in bows around the metal bit of the hanger, and you're done!

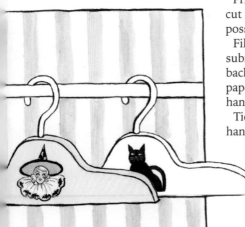

BROOM PLACE CARDS

MAKES 6

MATERIALS
bunches of natural raffia
6 x 17cm [6½in] wooden
  sticks (collect them from the
  woods or your local park)
1m [1yd] wire
enough card for 6 x 4cm
  [1½in] place cards
colour marker pens

EQUIPMENT
scissors
glue gun

These little place cards are so easy and inexpensive to make, but they look fantastic in a witches' tea party setting. Place one on top of each teacup and invite your coven over for afternoon tea. Dress code: black robe and pointy hat.

Take a clump of raffia, about 18cm [7in] long and fold it in the middle. Place the wooden stick inside it and secure with wire, right at the top, and a little bit lower too. Cut the raffia at the folded end to make it all equal length.
  Draw a ribbon-style banner on your card and colour it in with markers. It looks best if you leave some white bits to give it depth and a vintage look. Write the witch's name on the banner. Cut it to size, about 4cm [1½in], and attach it to the broomstick with a little glue. Repeat to make 5 more place cards.

SPOOKY DOOR WREATH ⁓

MAKES 1

MATERIALS
wire wreath frame (whichever
    size you want your wreath
    to be)
artificial silver pine Christmas
    garland (enough to cover
    your wire frame)
silver battery-operated wire
    lights (optional)
beaded spiderweb
beaded spider (see page 30)
a selection of artificial flower
    branches (pinks work really
    well with silver)
artificial hydrangeas
12- and 14-gauge wire
glass toadstool Christmas
    clip-on ornaments
ribbon

EQUIPMENT
scissors
wire cutters
glue gun (optional)

I have spoken before about the legend of the
Christmas spider (check out the Christmas Bauble
Chocolate Spiders on page 114). I am so obsessed
with this little story that I use it as an excuse to sneak
a spider into almost every Christmas project I make.
It is always done in a subtle way, so it doesn't take
away from the main theme of the project. In this
particular project we use techniques we have already
learned, such as the beaded spider (see page 30)
and incorporate them into a beautiful silver wreath.

Cover the wreath frame by wrapping the garland
around it and securing it with the silver wire. Use
excess branches to cover empty spots.
    If you would like to add wire lights, you would need
to add them at this stage using a glue gun. Attach the
battery box at the back so it remains hidden.
    Use the techniques described on page 30 to make
the beaded spider. To make the wire spiderweb, cut
3 strands of the thicker wire of a length that fits inside
the inner circle of your wreath frame. Overlay the 3
strands to create a 6-point star and secure them in the
centre with extra wire. Loop the thinner wire around
each arm of the star in concentric circles, inserting
tube-shaped beads between each loop. You could
also use just individual beads or just wire. Attach the
spiderweb and beaded spider to the internal top area
of the wreath using a little wire.
    Arrange your chosen flower branches and duplicate
them to attach them facing opposite ways on the
left-hand side of the wreath. Secure them with wire.
Glue some flower heads in between the branches –
I used artificial hydrangeas. Finally, clip on the glass
mushroom ornaments and attach a ribbon to the top
of the wreath.

WITCHMAS CRACKERS

MAKES 6

MATERIALS

CRACKERS
8 cardboard toilet rolls
3 sheets of black crêpe paper
3 sheets of orange crêpe paper
3m [3¼yd] metallic rickrack
    trim in orange
3m [3¼yd] metallic rickrack
    trim in black
6 cracker snaps
sticky tape
3m [3¼yd] orange ribbon
3m [3¼yd] black ribbon
trinkets of your choice
printed art deco witch and
    cat (download from www.
    witchesbyhelenagarcia.com/
    pages/downloads)
3 x A4 sheets of thin card
silver glitter glue

Last Christmas I made my own crackers for the
first time. It was so much fun and so easy that
I felt I needed to add it as a project here. Instead of
getting rubbish bits that will end up in the bin [trash],
you can fill them with really nice little trinkets, and
instead of those awful paper crowns, you can make a
fantastic-looking crown fit for a Grand High Witch.

To make 1 cracker, place 3 toilet rolls in a row on top of
a sheet of black or orange crêpe paper. Using them as
a guide, cut a piece of crêpe paper big enough to cover
the full cracker. Roll the 3 toilet rolls forward and wrap
them in the paper, securing with glue dots.
  Pull the 2 rolls at the sides slightly out of the paper
and scrunch the paper in the gap in order to create
creases. This is where you will tie the bows, on either
side of the central toilet roll. Before removing the end
rolls, attach 2 rows of rickrack trim to the both ends
of the crackers using the glue gun: black on the orange
crêpe ones and orange on the black ones. Remove the
side toilet rolls. Set the crackers aside.

FABRIC CROWNS
3.5m [3½yd] x 7cm [2¾in]
  wide gold Venise lace
1m [1yd] black grosgrain
  ribbon, for the ties
gold thread

EQUIPMENT
glue dots or glue gun
needle

To make the fabric crowns, simply measure your own head as a guide and cut a piece of the Venise lace 5–6cm [2–2½in] shorter, as you will have the ties to adjust to size. Cut the ribbon into 12 pieces about 8cm [3in] long. Fold each end of the Venise lace over the end of a length of ribbon twice, then pin and sew with the gold thread. Repeat to make the remaining 5 crackers.

Insert the cracker snaps into the crackers and secure with some sticky tape at both ends. Tie one end of the orange crackers with black ribbon, and the black crackers with orange ribbon. Then fill them with trinkets and the fabric crown, then tie the other end.

Print the images of the witch and the cat on to the thin card. Decorate the collar of the witch with the silver glitter glue. Cut them out and glue on to the crackers with a glue dot or using the glue gun.

HANGING PUMPKIN ORNAMENT

MAKES 1

MATERIALS
artificial pumpkin
PVA glue
biodegradable gold glitter
gold thread, for hanging
artificial leaves
dried fruit slices (like lemon,
    orange or apple)
artificial berries and/or
    flowers
cinnamon sticks
star anise
gold pipe cleaner

EQUIPMENT
paintbrush
glue gun

These lovely and glittery pumpkin ornaments make great drawer pulls in my house all year round. They are also wonderful Halloween decorations or Christmas tree ornaments. They look fabulous in gold or orange glitter, and the tops can be decorated with whatever you have at home. The plastic pumpkins are really easy to find, especially in the autumn, and you can make them in any size.

Remove the pumpkin stalk and set aside, then brush a thin layer of PVA glue all over the pumpkin. Work on the top half first, then turn it upside down and repeat.
   Sprinkle glitter all over, tapping the pumpkin several times to remove any excess, then leave to dry for 1 hour. You can do a second coat if you wish, but I quite like to see a bit of the orange showing underneath the glitter layer.
   Attach the gold thread: loop it around the stalk, reattaching it to the pumpkin with a little glue. Using the glue gun, attach the artificial leaves first, then arrange the rest of the items to your liking. Curl the pipe cleaner and attach it to the stalk with a little glue for the curly bits that usually come off the stalk. Use different decorations for different pumpkins.

SLEEPY VAMPIRE EASTER EGGS

MAKES 2

MATERIALS
2 large white eggs
about 240 ml [1 cup] hot
  water
1 tsp white wine vinegar
purple gel food colouring
black paint or marker
white paint or marker
red paint or marker
0.5m [½yd] ribbon
artificial white flowers
  (optional)

EQUIPMENT
glue gun

Using the old-fashioned way to dye Easter eggs but giving them a little spooky makeover, these are made to be hung on an Easter tree. If you're planning to eat the eggs, you could hard-boil them and paint them with food-grade colours, as the eggshells are porous.

Start by blowing out the eggs. Make a hole at the top and bottom of each egg with a skewer and blow out the contents into a bowl. Wipe the eggs clean.

Fill a glass with the hot water, then add the vinegar and a large dollop (about ¼ tsp) of purple food colouring. Mix well.

Place each eggshell in the glass and hold it down with a skewer for at least 5 minutes. The longer you leave it, the darker the colour will be. We are looking for a nice shade of violet for these. Remove the egg from the glass and leave it to dry completely, about 30 minutes, blowing out any water that may have got inside. Repeat with the other eggshell.

Once dry, using the paint or markers, draw the shape of the vampire's head and wings and colour it black. Draw the eyes, mouth and teeth with bits of blood.

Cut your chosen ribbon to whatever size you want it to be and loop it around, inserting both ends into the hole in the base of the egg. Secure with a little dot of glue. Glue a little flower onto the eggs, if liked, then hang on your Easter tree.

SCAREDY CAT WALL PLAQUE

MAKES 1

MATERIALS
oval wooden plaque, about
  20–22cm [8–8½in] long
mahogany wood stain
paper
2 packets Fimo clay
acrylic paints
screw-in eye
0.5m [½yd] grosgrain ribbon

EQUIPMENT
scissors
scalpel
paintbrush
glue gun

Believe it or not, I had never used Fimo clay before I created this project. This little piece of information is meant to inject some encouragement into anyone who may think they can't sculpt. The key is to use an image as a guide and to create depth by adding bits of clay in the right places.

Apply the mahogany wood stain to the wooden plaque. Give it 2 coats according to the manufacturer's instructions and leave it to dry fully between coats, about 1 hour.

On a piece of paper, draw a rough shape of a cat's head, using an image of a vintage Halloween cat as reference. Cut it out.

Roll out your Fimo clay until it is about 5mm [¼in] thick. Using your cat template, cut around it with your scalpel. Using the same cat image as reference, start moulding the features. Add clay to create cheeks, eyebrows, nose, etc., and scrape clay away from inside the ears and eyes. Create the whiskers with the scalpel. Keep marking all around to imitate hair.

For the ribbon, simply roll a strip of clay, cut 'V' shapes at each end and fold it into shape.

Preheat the oven to 90°C fan [225°F/Gas mark ¼] and line a baking sheet with greaseproof [wax] paper. Place the cat and ribbon on the lined baking sheet and bake according to the packet instructions. Remove from the oven and leave to cool for 10 minutes.

Once cooled, paint it. I painted the cat and ribbon black. Get creative with your colour choices – you could imitate the shades of your own cat and write their name on the ribbon.

To finish the plaque, screw the eye at the top and loop the ribbon through it. Tie a bow and hang.

OUIJA SERVING TRAY

MAKES 1

MATERIALS
1 laser-printed Ouija board
   template (download from
   www.witchesbyhelenagarcia.
   com/pages/downloads)
A4 waterslide decal paper
1 wooden or metal tray
   (preferably old/vintage)

EQUIPMENT
inkjet printer
setting spray

One of the key elements of this project is to find an old silver filigree tray, or even a wooden tray that looks the part. It's not hard, just look in charity shops [thrift stores] or online. I found a fair few that were suitable. Even oval wooden trays make a great Ouija board. The one I used had a broken tile base, so I went to the hardware store and bought a couple of tiles, cut them to size and replaced them. If using a wooden tray, you don't need to do any of that. I then designed the Ouija board in Photoshop and printed it onto waterslide decal paper. You may want to enlarge or reduce the design, depending on the size of your tray.

Print the Ouija board design onto a waterslide decal sheet using an inkjet printer.

Apply your first coat of setting spray and leave to dry for 15 minutes. Repeat this process 4 more times, letting the last one dry for a bit longer, or use a hairdryer to speed the process up.

Wipe the surface of the tray you are using. Make sure it is fully clean and dry.

Immerse your waterslide decal into a bowl of shallow water for 30–60 seconds. Peel off the backing paper and carefully place the Ouija decal on the surface of your tray. Smooth out the air bubbles and leave to dry for at least 3 hours.

If using a metal tray, you can preheat the oven to 100°C fan [250°F/Gas mark ½] and place the tray or tile inside for 10 minutes to speed up the drying time.

THE WITCH'S APOTHECARY

PUMPKIN SUGAR SCRUB

MAKES 1 X 250G [9OZ] JAR

2 Tbsp pumpkin purée,
   homemade (see method)
   or from a can
200g [1 cup] brown or pure
   cane sugar
2 Tbsp sweet almond oil
2–3 drops cinnamon essential
   oil

EQUIPMENT
food processor
latex gloves (optional)
250g [9oz] glass jar or
   container

Pumpkin is not only a delicious fruit, which also serves as a fabulous lantern to guide you through the darkness of winter, it is also full of nutrients that are beneficial for the skin and wonderfully soothing and moisturising for all skin types. This is a great recipe to use up any leftover pumpkin purée you may have, or you can make your own purée with pumpkin or butternut squash. Sugar scrubs are not only good for removing all those dead skin cells and allowing new skin to glow, but they also stimulate circulation and help even out skin tone.

If making your own pumpkin purée, preheat the oven to 180°C fan [400°F/Gas mark 6] and bake a large piece of unpeeled pumpkin or ½ butternut squash for 30 minutes. Scoop out the flesh into a food processor and process it into a purée. Allow to cool. Alternatively, use canned pumpkin.

In a medium bowl, mix all the ingredients well with clean hands or using latex gloves. Place the mixture in a 250g [9oz] jar and keep refrigerated until ready to use. It will keep for a month.

To use, apply the scrub all over your body and face in gentle circular movements and rinse well.

ELDERFLOWER BEAUTY WATER

I have an elder tree in my garden, so I make full use of its flowers and fruit and sometimes even the fungi that grow on it. If you live in the UK, elderflower is incredibly easy to come by. It's everywhere: in city parks, woodlands and in residential streets. I tend to use the flowers in the spring and the berries (which I much prefer) to make elderberry vinegar in the early autumn. Elderflower water makes a lovely toner, and it's particularly good for soothing the skin after being exposed to the sun.

MAKES 400ML [1¾ CUPS]

2 large heads elderflower
400ml [1¾ cups] boiling water
2 tsp vegetable glycerine

EQUIPMENT
muslin cloth [cheesecloth]
sterilised 400ml [14fl oz] bottle

Place the elderflower heads in a medium-sized heatproof bowl. Pour the boiling water over and cover with a lid or plate. Leave to infuse for 30 minutes.
  Strain into another bowl through muslin cloth [cheesecloth] to remove impurities. Add the glycerine and mix well.
  Pour into a sterilised 400ml [14fl oz] bottle and keep refrigerated for 2–3 weeks.

PEONY FACE TONER

The method for making this is exactly the same as the method for making rose water. While roses have been used in beauty treatments for thousands of years, peonies are less popular, even though they improve blood circulation, help against skin cracking in cold weather and possess soothing and anti-allergenic properties. And they are the most beautiful flower, although lacking in practical design as the heads of the peonies are so heavy the stems can't hold them. This is the reason I started making peony face toner: I wanted to make use of these blooms before they dropped to the ground in my garden. Now, I make it every year and apply it to my skin day and night. I use a deep pink peony, as it gives the toner a delicate natural pink colour and a gentle aroma.

MAKES 400ML [1¾ CUPS]

2 peony heads
1 tsp vodka

EQUIPMENT
muslin cloth [cheesecloth]
sterilised 400ml [14fl oz] bottle

Pull the petals off the peony heads and rinse them in fresh water to wash off any impurities. Place them in a large saucepan and pour in enough water to just cover them, about 500ml [2 cups]. Bring to a gentle simmer for about 30 minutes.
  Remove from the heat and strain through a muslin cloth [cheesecloth] into a bowl. Add the vodka and pour into a sterilised 400ml [14fl oz] bottle. Keep refrigerated for up to 10 days.

CHOCOLATE FACE MASK ～⁀

MAKES 1

3 Tbsp plain yogurt
½ vanilla pod [bean]
1 Tbsp raw organic cocoa
  powder
1 Tbsp rhassoul clay powder

The perfect activity for a witches' night in or out. This mask smells so delicious, you would want to eat it. I don't recommend you do, though. It will, however, leave you rejuvenated and ready to take your broom out for a ride. This mask is meant to be made to use fresh, so don't store it.

Place the yogurt in a small bowl, then split the vanilla pod in half lengthways and, using a sharp knife, scrape the seeds out into the bowl. Mix and leave to infuse for 30 minutes.

In a separate bowl, combine the cocoa powder and rhassoul clay powder. Add the infused yogurt, whisking until fully incorporated. The mixture should have a thick and creamy consistency. Feel free to add a little more yogurt if necessary.

Apply to a freshly washed face and neck. Leave for 10 minutes and rinse.

MA-SCARE-A REMOVER

MAKES ABOUT 80ML [⅓ CUP]

2 Tbsp castor oil
2 Tbsp extra virgin olive oil
2 Tbsp witch hazel

EQUIPMENT
80ml [2¾fl oz] spray bottle

This is one of the most useful products to make at home. It is quick, inexpensive and works so much better than any other make-up remover I have bought in the past 20 years. It only uses three ingredients. Witch hazel is a natural skin soother often used in aftershave formulas or to restore blistered or cracked skin. Castor oil, which is used in the manufacturing of soaps and lubricants, is a natural rejuvenator and olive oil has been used in beauty treatments for thousands of years. Feel free to double or triple the recipe.

Mix all the ingredients into a 80ml [2¾fl oz] spray bottle and shake well. Store for up to 12 months.
    To use, make sure you shake it each time, then spray onto a cotton pad and wipe your mascara away. I tend to use it to clean off all my make-up.

BEARD OIL

MAKES 4 X 20-ML [¾-FL OZ] BOTTLES

2 Tbsp jojoba oil
2 Tbsp sweet almond oil
2 Tbsp fractionated coconut oil
6–8 drops cedarwood essential oil
6–8 drops sandalwood essential oil

EQUIPMENT
small funnel
4 x 20-ml [¾-fl oz] bottles with droppers

Since 'witch' is a gender-inclusive term, here's one for the gents and some female witches too. This formula leaves beards soft and hydrated, with a wonderful musky aroma. The jojoba oil also strengthens the hair as it's non-allergenic and won't clog your pores or cause irritation. I strongly recommend using cedarwood essential oil, as it not only smells divine, it also adds shine to the hair. Beard oils can be seriously expensive to buy, so it's so worth witch-crafting your own. It also makes a fantastic present.

Mix all the ingredients well in a jug [measuring cup], then, using a small funnel, pour into 4 x 20ml [¾fl oz] bottles with droppers. Store for up to 6 months.

To apply, put a few drops onto your fingers and massage into your beard.

HEALTHY HAIR POTION ～⌒

MAKES 1 X 500ML [17FL OZ]
BOTTLE

1–2 geranium sprigs
  (including leaves and
  flowers)
2–3 lavender sprigs
1–2 rosemary sprigs
2–3 stinging nettle sprigs
a few firethorn sprigs with
  berries
peel of 1 lemon
500ml [2 cups] cider vinegar

EQUIPMENT
sterilised 500ml [17fl oz] jar
  or bottle

During my pregnancy, my hair looked incredible: thick, glossy and full of life. It was an unpleasant shock to then go through the worst hair-loss episode I have ever encountered, three months postpartum. I lost at least a third of my hair's volume. I searched far and wide for solutions and remedies. In the end I used all the information I had gathered to make my very own hair infusion, using plants and ingredients that have been scientifically proven to improve the look and volume of your hair. They are all ones I have available in the garden or are easy to forage from the woods. If out of season, omit the firethorn.

Place the geranium, lavender and rosemary sprigs in the sterilised jar or bottle. Add the nettles (using gloves) along with the firethorn sprigs and lemon peel. Fill the jar with the cider vinegar, making sure all plants are covered. Seal with the lid and leave to infuse in a warm place away from direct sunlight for 4 weeks, at which point the potion is ready to use.

To use, dilute 1 Tbsp in a cup of water, massage into your scalp while in the shower or bath before shampooing, then leave for 5 minutes before rinsing and washing your hair as normal. Store for 6–12 months.

CHARCOAL TEETH WHITENER

MAKES 1 X 50G [1¾OZ] TIN

2 Tbsp organic coconut oil
½ tsp activated charcoal
2 Tbsp bicarbonate of soda
[baking soda]
2 drops peppermint essential
oil

EQUIPMENT
50g [1¾oz] tin or airtight
container

Do not let the stories of witches having rotten teeth affect you. This natural toothpaste uses activated charcoal, which cleanses and whitens your teeth without abrasive chemicals. Mixing it with solid coconut oil also aids in reducing stains and plaque due to the oil's antibacterial properties. Let's keep those teeth bright as ghosts.

Place the coconut oil in a small heatproof bowl set over a pan of boiling water, making sure the base of the bowl doesn't touch the water, and leave to melt. Remove from the heat and add the activated charcoal, bicarbonate of soda and peppermint oil. Mix well until fully combined. Pour into a 50g [1¾oz] tin or airtight container and store in a cool, dark place for up to a month.

To use, simply dip your toothbrush into the mixture and brush your teeth in circular motions, then rinse off. Use 1–2 times per week.

WITCH HAZEL MOUTHWASH

MAKES 1 X 200ML [6¾FL OZ] BOTTLE

handful of fresh peppermint
  leaves
peel of ½ lemon
50ml [3½ Tbsp] boiling water
150ml [⅔ cup] witch hazel
30 drops peppermint essential
  oil
30 drops tea tree essential oil

EQUIPMENT
sterilised 200ml [6¾fl oz] jar
  or bottle

We cannot make a natural tooth cleaner and whitener without finishing our mouth health routine with an equally beneficial mouthwash. Instead of alcohol, this formula uses witch hazel, which won't dry out the mucous membranes in your mouth.

Place the peppermint leaves and lemon peel in a medium heatproof bowl and add the boiling water. Leave to steep for 30 minutes.

Strain through a sieve [strainer] into a jug [pitcher]. Add the witch hazel and essential oils. Stir well, pour into the sterilised jar or bottle and seal.

To use, add 1 Tbsp to a cup of cold water and rinse your mouth after brushing your teeth, then spit out. The blend will keep for 3 months.

SOLID PERFUME

MAKES 35ML [1¼OZ] SOLID
PERFUME

1 Tbsp beeswax or petroleum
  jelly
1 Tbsp sweet almond oil
10–15 drops of your favourite
  perfume

EQUIPMENT
containers of your choice

I have been collecting vintage cosmetics for quite
some time now, and although I mainly collect them
for the enchanting packaging, some items still have
plenty of use left in them. I am particularly talking
about the solid perfume containers here. Many of
them are wearable pieces of jewellery, like pendants
or brooches. All you need to do is make a fresh batch
of solid perfume to fill them with. What's more, you
can carry your favourite scent pinned to your jacket
or adorning your neck.

Melt the beeswax or petroleum jelly and almond oil
in a small heatproof bowl set over a pan of gently
simmering water, making sure the base of the bowl
doesn't touch the water. Remove from the heat, then
add a few drops or sprays from your favourite perfume
and mix well.
   Pour the mixture into your chosen containers and
leave to set. Store for 3–5 years.
   To apply, rub your finger gently on the solid perfume
and apply on the wrists and behind the ears.

LAVENDER SALVE

MAKES 10 X 30G [1OZ] TINS

40g [1 cup] dried lavender
 buds
270ml [1¼ cups] sweet
 almond, jojoba, vegetable or
 sunflower oil
3½ Tbsp beeswax pellets
1 Tbsp shea butter
15 drops lavender essential oil
4–5 drops lemon essential oil

EQUIPMENT
2 x sterilised 500ml [17fl oz]
 jars
muslin cloth [cheesecloth]
10 x 30g [1oz] tins or
 containers

I grow and harvest my own lavender at home; however, it is available everywhere and really easy to get hold of. Lavender is often associated with old ladies, but since I'm over 300 years old, I guess it suits me just fine. I love lavender, both as a cooking herb and as a cosmetic ingredient. The smell of lavender is scientifically proven to have a calming effect, releasing stress and helping you sleep better. Lavender salve is beneficial in so many ways: it moisturises and soothes cracked and itchy skin, and it can also help with skin irritations like eczema or even acne. I mainly use it as a lip balm for cracked lips in the winter months.

Put the lavender buds in a sterilised 500ml [17fl oz] jar. Pour in your chosen oil, making sure the buds are fully immersed. Get rid of any air bubbles, then put the lid on and give it a good shake. Leave in a warm spot but not in direct sunlight for 2 weeks, shaking it once a day. If you're not in a hurry, you could leave it for a few more weeks to carry on infusing.

Strain through a muslin cloth [cheesecloth] and store in another clean 500ml [17fl oz] glass jar until ready to use. The oil will keep for up to 1 year in a cool, dark cupboard.

To make the salve, place the lavender-infused oil and beeswax in a double boiler or in a heatproof bowl set over a pan of gently simmering water, making sure the base of the bowl doesn't touch the water. Stir constantly until the wax has melted. Remove from the heat and add the essential oils.

Pour into your chosen containers and leave to set completely before putting the lids on.

BIRTHSTONE LIP GLOSS ⟳

MAKES 13 X 6ML [⅕FL OZ] TUBES

55g [2oz] Versagel (lip gloss base)
25g [1oz] aloe vera oil flavoured oil (I used cherry)
13 small semi-precious stones
edible gold leaf/glitter or confetti

EQUIPMENT
perfume funnel
13 x 6ml [⅕fl oz] clear roll-on lip gloss tubes

This project is very much representative of my witchy teenage years when I was fascinated by horoscopes, astrology and magic. My birthstone is diamond, which would be a very expensive jewel to keep flooded with oils, so I used a semi-precious stone to go inside my lip gloss instead. Get creative with your lip gloss and add a selection of stones or foraged herbs.

Add the Versagel and aloe vera oils to a microwaveable container and heat at 30-second intervals in the microwave until they reach 37°C [98.6°F].

Mix well and add a few drops of your chosen flavoured oil. Using a perfume funnel, fill the clear roll-on lip gloss tubes a third of the way up. Add a stone to each, then fill to the top and add some edible gold leaf/glitter or confetti.

BAT BATH MELT

MAKES 6

285g [scant 1½ cups] bicarbonate of soda [baking soda]
140g [1 cup] citric acid
170g [¾ cup] cocoa butter, chopped
purple gel food colouring
1 tsp essential oil of your choice

EQUIPMENT
lollipop sticks
bat-shaped moulds

I used to make these cheeky melting bats for my shop. I always kept a few on the bathroom shelf as they are wonderfully moisturising, meaning you have one less job to do after your bath. I found the mould online: it's actually meant for chocolate, but it works perfectly fine for this project.

Place the lollipop sticks in the bat moulds. Sift the bicarbonate of soda and citric acid into a large bowl. Set aside.

Place the cocoa butter in a heatproof bowl set over a pan of boiling water, making sure the base of the bowl doesn't touch the water, and stir until melted. Remove from the heat and add a few drops of purple food colouring. It won't look incorporated yet, but the colour will develop when mixed in with the rest of the ingredients. Add the essential oil and mix well. Pour the wet ingredients into the dry and stir until fully mixed. Working quickly, pour the mixture into your bat moulds and leave to set completely for about 2–3 hours before unmoulding.

Drop one bat into a hot running bath. While it melts, you will see the nourishing oils rising to the surface. Use within 3–4 months.

PUMPKIN BATH BOMBS

MAKES 4

655g [3¼ cups] bicarbonate
  of soda [baking soda]
300g [2⅓ cups] citric acid
1 tsp cinnamon/apple
  fragrance oil
1 tsp sweet almond oil
orange powder food colouring
rose water (in spray bottle)
70g [⅓ cup] cocoa butter
biodegradable glitter and/or
  sprinkles

EQUIPMENT
latex gloves (optional)
bath bomb mould

In my very first book, I wrote that a sparkly pumpkin keeps witches clean so they can play on Halloween! These pumpkins bath bombs are actually an improved recipe from my original one. I've added a cocoa butter drizzle to add a moisturising element, and I've used powder colour so when you spray water on to your mixture, the colour magically changes. I found a pumpkin-shaped bath mould online, which I now stock in my shop www.witchesbyhelenagarcia.com, but a round one works too.

Sift 600g [3 cups] of the bicarbonate of soda and citric acid together into a large bowl. Add the fragrance oil and almond oil and mix in with your hands – I like to wear latex gloves for this. Sprinkle in about ½ tsp orange powder. Spray the rose water onto the mixture and watch it change colour. After a few sprays, mix it in with your hands and continue spraying until you get the right consistency.

To test the consistency, squeeze a handful of mixture in your hand and drop it back into the bowl. If it retains its shape when you drop it, then it is ready to use. If it breaks, it needs more water. We are looking for a powdery consistency like snow.

Fill both sides of the mould with your bath bomb mixture so they are overflowing. Press them together until they touch, removing any excess mixture from the sides. After 30 seconds or so, remove from the mould and place on a flat surface to dry for at least 24 hours. Repeat with the remaining mixture.

Once the pumpkins are ready, melt the cocoa butter in a medium-sized heatproof bowl set over a pan of gently simmering water, making sure the base of the bowl doesn't touch the water. Mix in the remaining bicarbonate of soda: you should get a consistency that's right for drizzling, but if you don't, simply adjust the amounts. Using a spoon, drizzle the mixture over the bath bombs, then sprinkle your glitter or chosen sprinkles on top. Store for up to 6 months.

VICTORIAN MUSTARD BATH

MAKES ABOUT 275G [1 CUP]

275g [1¾ cups] bicarbonate
of soda [baking soda]
4 Tbsp mustard powder
4 drops peppermint essential
oil
2 drops eucalyptus essential
oil

EQUIPMENT
airtight container

The Victorians were on to something when they
formulated the warming wonders of mustard
baths. However, the use of mustard in this way can
be traced back to ancient Greece. It's perfect for
relieving those aches and pains associated with a
winter cold or flu. The mustard bath was a bestseller
in my first apothecary shop in Leeds, and now I make
it at home for personal use.

In a medium bowl, sift the bicarbonate of soda and
mustard powder together. Add the essential oils
and mix well with clean hands. Store in an airtight
container.
To use, simply add ½ cup to a hot running bath and
enjoy. I sometimes mix in some Epsom salts too.

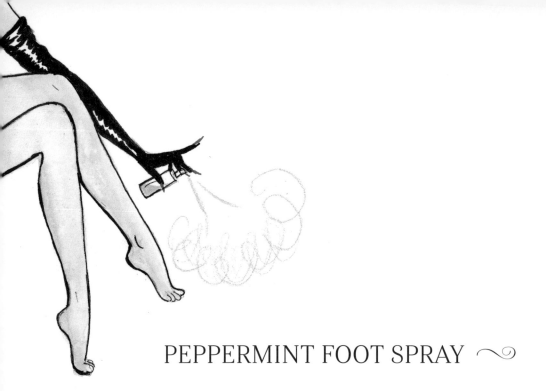

PEPPERMINT FOOT SPRAY ∽

MAKES 100ML [3½FL OZ]

75ml [⅓ cup] distilled water
12 drops peppermint essential
  oil
12 drops tea tree essential oil
25ml [2 Tbsp] witch hazel

EQUIPMENT
100ml [3½fl oz] spray bottle

This is a wonderful, refreshing and soothing spray for your witchy feet. It's one of those formulas I have handwritten in a little notebook. It's perfect to carry in your handbag in the summer months to give your hot, tired feet an uplifting spray. The peppermint and tea tree essential oils possess antibacterial properties, helping you keep your claws nice and fresh.

Fill your spray bottle three-quarters of the way up with distilled water. Add the peppermint and tea tree essential oils and top up with the witch hazel. Store for up to 6 months. Shake well before use.

To apply, simply spray the soles of your feet and between your toes. Leave for a few minutes, then put your socks on.

APOTHECARY CANDLES

MAKES 1 X 250G [9OZ]
CANDLE

1 wick with a metal base (long
  enough to fit your chosen
  container)
350g [2/3 cup] soy wax flakes
30 drops cinnamon leaf
  essential oil
20 drops orange essential oil
10 drops clove bud essential
  oil

EQUIPMENT
glue gun
250g [9oz] apothecary-style
  jar
candle label (download from
  www.witchesbyhelenagarcia.
  com/pages/downloads)
adhesive paper

Making your own candles is a magical experience.
You get to choose the scents, type of wax and wick,
and the container you'd like it to be in. In this case,
an amber apothecary-style jar. For this recipe, I've
chosen winter scents, but you can use whatever
essential oils you fancy. I've also opted for soy wax
to make the candles suitable for vegans and
generally less harmful.

To attach your wick, squirt a little glue from your
glue gun to the underside of the metal base of the
candle wick and stick it in the bottom of the apothecary
jar. I sometimes use a skewer to press it down. Make
sure the wick is straight – you can use a wooden peg to
help with this.
  Place the soy wax flakes in a medium heatproof bowl
set over a pan of gently simmering water, making sure
the base of the bowl doesn't touch the water, and stir
until completely melted. Remove from the heat and
leave to cool slightly before adding the essential oils.
Pour into your container and leave to set.
  Once it sets, the candle is ready to use. To finish the
candle, print the label onto adhesive paper, then cut
it out and stick it onto the glass. I've left space
at the bottom for you to write the date, your
name or the name of whoever you are gifting
the candle to.

'EVERY DAY IS HALLOWEEN' ROOM SPRAY ⁓

MAKES 100ML [3½FL OZ]

75ml [⅓ cup] distilled water
30 drops pumpkin spice
   fragrance oil
25ml [2 Tbsp] witch hazel

EQUIPMENT
100ml [3½fl oz] spray bottle

This was a very popular product in my apothecary shop back in the day, specially formulated for those of us who wish every day was Halloween. This room spray is obviously scented with pumpkin spice fragrance oil. Spray it around the house to feel like you're in October any time of the year.

Add the distilled water to a 100ml [3½fl oz] spray bottle. Mix in the pumpkin spice fragrance oil, then top with the witch hazel and shake well. Store in a cool, dry place.

THE WITCH'S CAULDRON

BONE BREADSTICKS

MAKES 16

¾ tsp black food colouring
  or charcoal powder
185ml [¾ cup] lukewarm
  water, about 40°C [104°F]
380g [2¾ cups] strong white
  bread flour, plus extra for
  dusting
1 tsp instant dried yeast
60ml [¼ cup] olive oil
2 Tbsp unsalted butter, melted
  and slightly cooled, plus
  100g [7 Tbsp], melted, for
  brushing
1½ tsp table salt
100g [¾ cup] poppy seeds
Boo Boo Ghanoush (page 88),
  to serve

EQUIPMENT
electric stand mixer
pizza cutter
ball moulding tool

When I was on the *Great British Bake Off*, I made
bone and snake breadsticks to accompany some
showstopper loaves during bread week. This time
the soft and buttery bones are the star of the show.
I coloured them slightly grey using some ink
I extracted from inkcap mushrooms, but unless
you know exactly what you're doing I would
recommend you use a little charcoal powder or
black food colouring.

Mix the black food colour or charcoal into the warm
water and set aside.

Add the bread flour, yeast, coloured water, olive oil,
2 Tbsp butter and salt to an electric stand mixer fitted
with a dough hook attachment and mix on low speed
until fully incorporated. Increase the speed to medium–
low and knead the dough for 5 minutes. Cover the
bowl with clingfilm [plastic wrap] and leave the dough
to rise in a warm place for 1 hour, or until doubled
in size.

Preheat the oven to 190°C fan [410°F/Gas mark 6½]
and line 2 baking sheets with baking paper or a silicone
mat.

Place the dough on a floured surface and cut it in half.
Roll out the first half to a thickness of about 1cm [½in]
until you have a 25-cm [10-in] long rectangle. Using a
pizza cutter, cut the dough into 8 long, thin strips.

Shape the strips into bones by rolling them into
cylinders with your hands and pressing on the ends to
create a 'ball' shape, then dent it with a ball moulding
tool or using your thumb. For others, try shaping the
dough into a knot at the ends. Repeat this process with
the remaining dough. Place the bones on the lined
baking sheets.

Brush the breadsticks with the melted butter and
sprinkle with the poppy seeds, then bake for 20–25
minutes. Transfer the breadsticks to a wire rack and
leave to cool. Serve with the Boo Boo Ghanoush.

BOO BOO GHANOUSH ∽

SERVES 4-6

2 aubergines [eggplants]
95ml [⅓ cup] extra virgin
  olive oil, plus extra for
  drizzling
2–3 garlic cloves, minced
juice of ½ lemon
55g [¼ cup] tahini
large pinch of salt, or to taste
pinch of ground cumin
1 tsp smoked paprika, plus
  extra for dusting
Bone Breadsticks (page 86),
  to serve

I love aubergines [eggplants]. They are, without doubt, among my favourite vegetables: fried, baked, but mostly made into this Eastern Mediterranean dip. I have absolutely no shame in admitting I eat this ghanoush by the spoonful, although you may want to use the Bone Breadsticks (page 86) to dip into it. The quantities of each ingredient are a guide, as you may want to adjust according to your taste. I like it with quite a lot of smoked paprika.

Preheat the oven to 200°C fan [425°F/Gas mark 7] and line a large baking tray with baking paper.
  Cut the aubergines in half lengthways, then drizzle with a little olive oil and bake, skin-side up, for 40 minutes, or until very tender.
  Leave the aubergine halves to cool for a few minutes, then scoop the flesh out with a spoon. Place in a sieve [strainer] over a bowl and press down with the spoon to remove as much liquid as you can.
  Place the aubergine flesh in a clean bowl and add the remaining ingredients. Mix well with a fork in order to break down the flesh, then taste and adjust the lemon, garlic and seasoning. Serve alongside the Bone Breadsticks.

BREAD TOADS

MAKES 8

2½ tsp instant dried yeast
250ml [1 cup] milk, lukewarm
560g [4¼ cups] strong white
   bread flour, plus extra for
   dusting
2 tsp salt
2 Tbsp caster [granulated]
   sugar
60g [¼ cup] unsalted butter,
   softened
2 large eggs
green gel food colouring
brown gel food colouring
yellow gel food colouring
black food paint
200g [7oz] shop-bought royal
   icing

EQUIPMENT
electric stand mixer
kitchen scissors
piping [pastry] bags

Toads and toadstools are highly poisonous (the word 'toad' refers to poison in Old English), and often associated with witches. These toads, however, are made with an enriched dough that is not too sweet, so they can easily be enjoyed as an accompaniment to a savoury meal or just as they are. Or you can make them live up to their name and use them as a decoy to poison your worst enemy.

In a medium bowl, sprinkle the yeast over the lukewarm milk and leave for a few minutes.

Mix the flour, salt and sugar in an electric stand mixer fitted with a dough hook attachment. Add the milk and yeast, along with the butter, eggs and green food colouring and continue kneading for about 5 minutes, or until the dough comes away from the sides and is nice and smooth. Cover the bowl with a damp tea towel and leave to rise in a warm place for 1–1½ hours until doubled in size.

Line a large baking sheet with baking paper. Turn the dough onto a lightly floured surface and knock the air out by kneading it for a few seconds, then divide into 8 equal pieces.

To shape the dough into toads, take one of the dough pieces and remove about a third for the limbs. Working on the lined baking sheet, form the body into an oval with one end narrower than the other. The wider end will be the rear part of the toad.

Divide the remaining dough in half, then divide one of these pieces in half again. Roll into a tube shape that's thicker at one end, and shape it to form a thigh and leg for the toad's back leg. Use scissors to cut three toes into the foot. Repeat to make the other back leg.

Divide the remaining dough into three. Form two of these pieces into front legs for the toad, again shaping the toes with scissors. Cut the last piece in half and roll it into two balls. Place on either side of the face for the bulgy eyes.

cont …

Repeat with the remaining dough to make 8 toads.

Cover with a damp tea towel and leave to prove at room temperature for 30 minutes .

Preheat the oven to 200°C fan [425°F/Gas mark 7].

When you are ready to bake, you can use your thumb to pinch nostril shapes into the toads' faces, and a sharp knife to give them mouths, but it not necessary. Bake for 16–18 minutes. Leave to cool completely on a wire rack before decorating.

To decorate your toads, colour some royal icing in dark green, some in brown and some in yellow. Use the green icing to create 'warts' on the back and thighs, then pipe smaller bumps in brown and yellow. You can also use the yellow to draw a line along the spine and around the eyelids. Paint the eyes in black.

You can get creative with the design or use a toad picture as reference and make it accurate. I actually boiled a kettle and used the steam to make the royal icing run a little, which gave the toads a bit of an abstract look.

PIRANHA FISH PIE ⌒◦

SERVES 2

MASHED POTATOES
600g [1lb 5oz] potatoes, such
  as Yukon Gold, peeled and
  chopped into small pieces
2 Tbsp butter
4 Tbsp crème fraîche
2 tsp Dijon mustard
salt and pepper

FILLING
1 Tbsp butter
1 shallot, chopped
1 Tbsp plain [all-purpose]
  flour, plus extra for dusting
200ml [¾ cup plus 1 Tbsp]
  fish stock
3 Tbsp crème fraîche
½ tsp Dijon mustard
freshly grated nutmeg, to taste
2 Tbsp chopped dill
salt and pepper
250g [9oz] packet mixed
  fish (salmon, cod, smoked
  haddock), cut into 2cm
  [¾in] pieces
40g [⅓ cup] frozen petits pois
2 sheets store-bought
  shortcrust pastry
1 egg, beaten, for egg wash

EQUIPMENT
potato ricer or steel moulin,
  or electric stand or handheld
  mixer
piping [pastry] bag
2 x 12 x 9.5cm [4½ x 3¾in]
  ovenproof casserole dishes

I was terrible with fish as a child: no matter how it was presented to me, I plainly refused to eat it. My parents assured me I would change my mind and would like it as an adult. It didn't happen. My child, however, loves fish and fish pie and even before she could walk, she had eaten sophisticated foods you wouldn't expect a young kid to enjoy. I developed this recipe with her in mind. Incidentally, my neighbours have also tried this piranha pie, which they absolutely loved. I used individual oval-shaped casserole dishes for this recipe.

Preheat the oven to 200°C fan [425°F/Gas mark 7].
  Cook the potatoes in a saucepan of boiling salted water until soft. Drain, return to the pan and add the butter, crème fraîche and mustard, and season to taste. Use a potato ricer or steel moulin to mash the potatoes, or if you don't have either, then use an electric stand mixer fitted with a paddle attachment or a handheld mixer. Spoon into a piping [pastry] bag and set aside.
  To make the sauce, melt the butter in a deep frying pan over a medium heat and sauté the shallot for 4–5 minutes until soft and translucent. Stir in the flour to make a roux. Using a whisk, gradually whisk in the fish stock. Cook until it thickens, whisking constantly to avoid lumps forming. Remove from the heat and stir in the crème fraîche, mustard, nutmeg and dill. Season with salt and pepper.
  Divide the fish equally between the casserole dishes, then add the peas and pour over the sauce. Pipe a layer of mashed potato over the top, then smooth over with a palette knife, creating a dome. Set aside while you make the pastry decorations.

cont …

Roll out the pastry on a lightly floured surface until it is 3mm [⅛in] thick. To make the head of the piranha, create the general shape with foil. My head was 7.5cm [3in] wide. Cover with the pastry and create the eyes and eyelids, and teeth (just bottom teeth). Add some 'warts' all around the face.

Cut out the side and top fins from the pastry with a sharp knife and score them vertically. For the scales, cut out 3cm [1¼in] diameter circles and score them with your knife.

Place the head, scales and fins on separate baking trays and brush with egg. Bake the head and pies for 25–30 minutes, and the fins and scales for about 15–20 minutes. Keep an eye on them so they don't burn. Arrange the pastry pieces on top of the mashed potato to create your piranha and serve.

FLYING SAUSAGE PIE

MAKES 12

PASTRY
500g [3¾ cups] plain [all-
  purpose] flour, plus extra
  for dusting
2 scant tsp salt
250g [1 cup plus 2 Tbsp] cold
  unsalted butter, cubed
2 medium egg yolks, plus
  2 extra yolks, beaten, for
  brushing
7–8 Tbsp ice-cold water

FILLING
455g [1lb] good-quality pork
  sausages
150g [¾ cup] roasted red
  peppers from a jar, well
  drained, patted dry and
  chopped
finely grated zest of
  1 unwaxed lemon
½ tsp mustard seeds, crushed
1 Tbsp tomato purée [paste]
salt and pepper
handful of redcurrants

EQUIPMENT
5cm [2in] round cutter
9cm [3½in] round cutter
piping nozzle
bubble straw

I've made cookie flying saucers before, but I thought
it would be interesting to try a savoury version. The
sausage, roasted pepper and lemon filling is honestly
divine. I use it to make sausage rolls all the time, and
sometimes I just cook it on its own like mince in a
frying pan [skillet]: I highly recommend it. I've tried
making these with shop-bought pastry, but they just
lose shape, so it's best to make your own.

On a clean surface, combine the flour and salt. Add
the butter and rub it between your fingers until it
resembles breadcrumbs. Alternatively, use a food
processor.

Make a well in the centre and add the egg yolks and
water (you may not need all the water). Mix by hand
and bring the dough together to form a smooth ball.
Wrap in clingfilm [plastic wrap] and refrigerate for
30 minutes.

Line 2 baking trays with silicone mats or baking
paper.

Cut the sausages lengthways, remove the meat and
add to a mixing bowl. Add the peppers, lemon zest,
mustard seeds and tomato purée, and season with
salt and pepper. Mix well with your hands until all the
ingredients have come together.

Roll the dough out on a lightly floured surface
until it is 3mm [⅛in] thick. Cut out 2 x 9cm [3½in]
circles, then roll them thinner with your rolling pin,
maintaining the round shape. Spoon 1 heaped Tbsp
of the filling into the centre of one circle, then dip your
fingers in a little water and wet the dough around the
pork mixture.

Top with the other circle and smooth the pastry out,
creating a dome in the centre. Seal the dome with a
5cm [2in] round cutter, then trim the whole structure
with an 9cm round cutter for a second time to create
a neat, round shape.

cont …

Using a piping nozzle, cut out 8 small circles from the dough, then cut a smaller circle in the middle of each one (I used a bubble straw for the inner circle). Attach them around the flying saucer in a circle with a little water. These will hold the lights (redcurrants). Repeat the process with the rest of the dough and filling to make 12 pies in total.

Place the pies on the lined baking trays and refrigerate them for 10 minutes or so.

Preheat the oven to 180°C fan [400°F/Gas mark 6].

Take the pies out of the fridge, prick a few holes on the base with a toothpick and brush them with the beaten egg yolk. Make a hole in the top so steam can escape. Place the redcurrants in the 'lights' settings and bake for 30 minutes, or until golden brown. Serve immediately or store in the fridge for 3–4 days.

SOPA DE MUERTOS
(SOUP OF THE DEAD)

SERVES 4

2 Tbsp butter
2 Tbsp olive oil, plus extra
  for brushing
6 shallots, chopped
2 garlic cloves, minced
500g [10 cups] mixed
  mushrooms, such as button,
  porcini, shiitake and oyster,
  chopped into equal pieces,
  plus 2–3 button mushrooms,
  left whole
salt and pepper
a few thyme sprigs
2 Tbsp white wine
1 Tbsp cornflour [cornstarch]
½ tsp porcini powder
1 litre [4 cups] chicken or
  vegetable stock
5 Tbsp single [light] cream
truffle oil, to serve

EQUIPMENT
food processor or immersion
  blender
straw

I was tagged on a social media post showing some fried 'skull' mushrooms last October by almost everyone I knew, and many I've never met. I got the message, and I developed a glorious recipe from it. This is a wild mushroom soup to truly die for. Made with a combination of foraged and shop-bought mushrooms, you can easily make it with the 'wild' varieties sold in supermarkets. I make my own porcini powder, but it is also available online. I really recommend you use it, as well as the truffle oil. as it takes this soup to another level.

Preheat the oven to 180°C fan [400°F/Gas mark 6].
  Place the butter and oil in a large pan over a low–medium heat, then add the shallots and garlic and cook for 10 minutes, or until soft and translucent. Add the mushrooms, except for the button mushrooms, to the pan. Season with salt and pepper, add a couple of thyme sprigs and cook for 5 minutes. Add the wine and cook for a further 1–2 minutes. Remove a couple of the chopped mushrooms and set aside for the garnish.
  Sprinkle in the cornflour and porcini powder, stir to combine, then add the chicken stock. Bring to the boil, then reduce the heat and simmer for 10 minutes.
  Meanwhile, carve skull shapes out of the whole button mushrooms using a sharp knife for the teeth and nose and a straw to cut out the eye sockets. Place them on a baking tray, brush with oil and bake in the oven for 15 minutes.
  Pour the soup into a food processor, or use an immersion blender, and blitz until smooth. Stir in the single cream. Serve the soup with the skulls, reserved mushrooms, remaining thyme sprigs and a drizzle of truffle oil.

WHEEL OF THE YEAR
TURKEY AND CHORIZO PIE ⌁

SERVES 6

PASTRY
500g [3¾ cups] plain [all-
    purpose] flour, plus extra
    for dusting
2 scant tsp salt
250g [1 cup plus 2 Tbsp] cold
    unsalted butter, cubed
2 medium egg yolks, plus
    1 extra yolk, beaten, for
    brushing
100ml [7 Tbsp] ice-cold water
black edible ink pen

FILLING
2 Tbsp olive oil
4–5 shallots, chopped
2 garlic cloves, chopped
½ chorizo sausage, chopped
    into small pieces
600g [4 cups] leftover turkey
    meat or boneless chicken
    thighs, chopped
salt and pepper
2 tsp paprika
½ tsp Cajun seasoning
50ml [3½ Tbsp] sherry
1 Tbsp cornflour [cornstarch]
500ml [2 cups] chicken stock
150ml [⅔ cup] single [light]
    cream

EQUIPMENT
24cm [9½in] pie dish

This is the perfect dish for a Thanksgiving dinner
or a Boxing Day meal using leftover turkey. It
also works really well with chicken thighs, as the
dominant flavour of this dish comes from the chorizo
and paprika. This is one of those recipes you make
up in order to use leftovers, but it turns out better
than the original meal. I thought it would be fun
to decorate it as a wheel of the year to mark the
seasonal festivals. I used cookie cutters and moulds
I had at home, but I also moulded some of the
decorations by hand.

On a clean surface, combine the flour and salt. Add
the butter and rub it between your fingers until it
resembles breadcrumbs. Alternatively, use a food
processor.
　Make a well in the centre, add the egg yolks and the
ice-cold water, then mix by hand to bring the dough
together to form a smooth ball. Divide in half, wrap in
clingfilm [plastic wrap] and refrigerate for 30 minutes.
　Heat the oil in a large pan over a low–medium heat.
Add the shallots and garlic and fry for 5–6 minutes.
Add the chorizo and cook for a further 2–3 minutes.
　Add the turkey or chicken and cook until golden
brown. Season with salt, pepper, paprika and Cajun
spice. Add the sherry and cook for 1 minute, or until
the alcohol has evaporated a little.
　Sprinkle over the cornflour, then stir through and
add the stock. Bring to the boil, then reduce the heat
and simmer for a few minutes until it thickens a little.
Remove from the heat, check the seasoning and adjust,
if necessary. Add the cream.
　Preheat the oven to 180°C fan [400°F/Gas mark 6].

cont …

Roll out the dough on a lightly floured surface. Place a 24cm [9½in] pie dish upside down on the dough and cut around it. Repeat this so that you have 2 dough circles. Take one circle and cut a smaller one out of the middle (by eye, or by cutting around a smaller plate) so that you're left with an empty wheel – this will be where you write the pagan festival name. Dip your finger in a little water and rub it around the edge of the circle, then lay the wheel on top and press gently to stick it in place.

Pour the filling into your pie dish and top with the dough circles.

Cut out a small circle from the remaining dough, around 3cm [1¼in] in diameter, and place it in the middle of pie top. Then use 5mm [¼in] strips of pastry to divide the wheel into 8 sections. This will give you the 8 areas to decorate according to the festival.

Decorate them as you wish. I made a moon, stars and some holly leaves for Yule, a candle and some florals for Imbolc, the Green Man for Ostara, a bonfire for Beltane, the sun for Litha, crops for Lammas, autumnal leaves and a pumpkin for Mabon and a crow skull for Samhain.

Place the pie in the freezer for 10 minutes to make sure the butter in the pastry hardens again. Remove and brush with the beaten egg yolk and bake for 25–30 minutes until golden brown. Serve immediately.

'DING DONG, THE WITCH IS DEAD' PASTA ∽

SERVES 6

SOMBRERONI PASTA
150g [1 cup plus 4 tsp] '00'
  pasta flour
½ tsp activated charcoal
  powder
2 large eggs
1 tsp olive oil
½ tsp salt

FILLING
75g [2½oz] feta cheese
2 garlic cloves, minced
75g [¾ cup] grated Pecorino
  cheese
handful of basil leaves, finely
  chopped
salt and pepper

SAUCE
4 garlic cloves, crushed
2 Tbsp olive oil
400g [8 cups] spinach
juice of ½ lemon
2 Tbsp grated Parmigiano-
  Reggiano cheese
100ml [7 Tbsp] single [light]
  cream
salt and pepper

EQUIPMENT
food processor
rolling pin or pasta machine
9.5cm [3¾in] ring cutter
7cm [2¾in] ring cutter

I'm sure you've heard of ravioli or tortellini, but have you ever heard of a pasta shape called sombreroni? If you haven't, they are little (or large in this case) hat-shaped pasta pieces. As soon as I thought of sombreroni, I had an image of the Wicked Witch of the West melting in liquid leaving only her pointy black hat behind. This is how the dish was born.

To make the pasta, add the flour, charcoal powder, eggs, oil and salt to a food processor and pulse a few times until the mixture resembles breadcrumbs. Add a little water, if necessary.

Tip the dough onto a clean surface and bring it together with your hands to form a ball. Knead it for 2 minutes until smooth. Add flour if necessary: we are looking for a dry dough. Wrap the dough in clingfilm [plastic wrap] and leave to rest at room temperature for 20–30 minutes.

Prepare the filling by crumbling the feta cheese into a large bowl, then add the garlic, Pecorino cheese and basil and season to taste. You can add some oregano or other herbs too. Mix well.

To make the sombreroni pasta shapes, roll the dough out by hand using a rolling pin or with a pasta machine. I have done it both ways and it works either way: it just needs to be around 2mm [1/16in] thick, and the surface needs to be well floured.

Cut out 3 x 9.5cm [3¾in] diameter circles, then cut each circle in half. This will give you 6 semicircles. Hold one semicircle horizontally and bring both ends together to create a cone, pressing them so they stick together. Repeat with the rest of the semicircles. These will be the hat tops.

For the hat brims, cut out another 6 circles, about 7cm [2¾in] in diameter.

cont …

Preheat the oven to 180°C fan [400°F/Gas mark 6], line a large baking sheet with baking paper and bring a large pan of salted water to the boil.

Cook the sombreroni brims in the boiling water for 7 minutes, then remove them with a slotted spoon and transfer to a plate. Add the cones and boil for 6 minutes. Drain, keeping about ½ cup of the cooking water for the sauce, and set aside.

Place the sombreroni brims on the lined baking sheet. Fill the pasta cones with the feta mixture and place on top of the brims. Brush with olive oil and bake for 10 minutes.

To make the sauce, sauté the garlic in the olive oil over a medium heat for 3–4 minutes until soft, then add the spinach and cook for another 2–3 minutes. Transfer the mixture to a food processor, add the lemon juice, Parmigiano cheese and ½ cup or so of the pasta water and blitz until smooth. Add the cream, then taste and season.

Pour the sauce onto 6 plates and place a filled witch hat in the middle while screeching to yourself, 'I'm melting!'

CAULDRON CHEESEBALL

A few years ago there was a video doing the rounds of how to make a cheese cauldron. It is such a perfect goodie to present on a Ouija board to call on the cheese spirits. Use it as an appetiser or for the end of a meal séance. The chive crackers are perfect accompaniments.

SERVES 4

225 g [1 cup] cream cheese, plus extra 85g [⅓ cup] for the rim
115g [1¼ cups] grated mature [sharp] Cheddar cheese
1 spring onion [scallion], finely chopped
bunch of chives, finely chopped
½ tsp Worcestershire sauce
½ tsp Tabasco
pinch of garlic powder
ground black pepper
100g [¾ cup] poppy seeds
guacamole, to serve
a few breadsticks, for burning wood
yellow and red [bell] pepper strips, for flames

EQUIPMENT
piping [pastry] bag

In a bowl, stir the cream cheese, Cheddar, spring onion, chives, Worcestershire sauce, Tabasco, garlic powder and pepper with a wooden spoon. Roll into a ball, then cover and refrigerate for 10 minutes.

Put the poppy seeds in a shallow bowl and roll the chilled cheeseball in them, leaving the top third uncovered.

Beat the 85g [⅓ cup] cream cheese until smooth. Spoon into a piping bag, cut the end and pipe onto the rim of the cauldron. Cover in poppy seeds.

Place some breadsticks in the middle of a plate and put the cauldron on top. Stick the pepper strips to the base with cream cheese. Pipe some guacamole inside.

CHIVE BLOSSOM & GOAT CHEESE CRACKERS

Chive flowers are so underrated, I love to use them in my cooking or to infuse vinegar. They have such a wonderful flavour. They work perfectly in these crackers, which are incredibly simple to make and are the ideal accompaniment to the Cauldron Cheeseball.

MAKES 16-20

100g [¾ cup] goat cheese, softened
2 Tbsp unsalted butter, softened
120g [1 cup minus 1½ Tbsp] plain [all-purpose] flour
4 chive blossoms, petals only

EQUIPMENT
spiderweb cookie cutter

Cream the cheese, butter and flour together in a medium bowl with a wooden spoon. Add the flower petals and combine until you get a dough-like consistency. Roll into a log, cover in clingfilm [plastic wrap] and refrigerate for 1 hour.

Preheat the oven to 200°C fan [425°F/ Gas mark 7].

Slice the log into 5mm [¼in] discs, then stamp with a spiderweb cookie cutter and bake for 12–14 minutes. Remove from the oven and leave to cool on a wire rack. These will keep in the fridge for 5–6 days.

GREEN MAN NETTLE AND LEMON CAKE

SERVES 4-6

135g [4¾oz] pack blackberry
  jelly cubes, or enough jello
  powder for 1 pint liquid
black gel food colouring
non-stick cooking spray
100g [1 cup] nettle leaves
  (pick the ones on the top
  10cm [4in] of the plant)
200g [¾ cup plus 2 Tbsp] cake
  margarine (I used Stork)
160g [¾ cup plus 1 Tbsp]
  caster [granulated] sugar
3 large eggs
1 tsp vanilla extract
grated zest of 2 unwaxed
  lemons and juice of 1
250g [1¾ cups plus 2 Tbsp]
  self-raising flour
½ tsp salt
500g [1⅔ cups] marzipan
green food colouring
edible bronze lustre dust

LEMON BUTTERCREAM
125g [½ cup plus 1 Tbsp]
  butter, at room temperature
250g [1¾ cups] icing
  [confectioners'] sugar, sifted
grated zest of 2 unwaxed
  lemons and juice of ½

DRIZZLE
4 Tbsp icing [confectioners']
  sugar
juice of 2 large lemons

EQUIPMENT
24 semi-sphere silicone mould
  with 3cm [1¼in] diameter
  holes
2 x 20cm [8in] round
  sandwich tins
food processor
electric stand mixer
ball modelling tool
leaf cookie cutters

I made this cake for a friend last spring. I had just picked some fresh nettle leaves and the idea came to me while walking back home with my wolfdog and wicker basket in hand. The nettles don't just give this cake a depth of flavour, they also add a wonderful natural colour and an abundance of nutrients. Is there such thing as healthy cake? I believe so.

First, make the eyes. Follow the packet instructions to make the blackberry jelly, then add some black gel food colouring to the mixture to make it darker and pour it into a 24 semi-sphere silicone mould. You'll only need 2 for the eyes, so snack on the others.

Preheat the oven to 170°C fan [375°F/Gas mark 5] and spray 2 x 20cm [8in] round sandwich tins with non-stick cooking spray.

Wearing rubber gloves, wash the nettle leaves, then blanch them in a pan of boiling water for 3–4 minutes. This will remove the sting. Drain well, squeezing the water out with your hands, and blitz in a food processor until smooth.

In an electric stand mixer fitted with a paddle attachment, beat the margarine and caster sugar together until light and fluffy. Add the eggs, one at a time, mixing well between each addition, then add the nettles, vanilla and the zest of 2 lemons and the juice of one. Mix in the flour and salt and continue mixing until fully combined.

Divide the batter between the prepared tins and bake for 25–30 minutes until a skewer inserted into the middle comes out clean. Remove from the oven and leave to cool slightly in the tins.

Meanwhile, to make the lemon buttercream, beat the butter in an electric stand mixer on medium speed until pale and fluffy. Reduce the speed to low and slowly add the icing sugar. Add the lemon zest and juice and continue mixing until fully combined. Set aside.

cont …

To make the lemon drizzle, put the sugar and lemon juice in a saucepan over a medium heat. Once the sugar has dissolved, cook for a few minutes or until it develops a syrupy consistency. Remove from the heat and set aside.

Using a sharp knife, level one of the cakes and leave the other one with a dome. This will help to give depth to the Green Man's face. Poke both cakes in various places with a skewer, then spoon the sugar syrup over the top while still warm. Leave to cool a little more.

Spread a layer of buttercream over the levelled cake and top with the domed cake layer. Brush a little of the syrup all over the top of the cake so the marzipan has something to stick to.

Mix the green colour into the marzipan and knead until it is fully incorporated. I recommend using gloves for this. Mould a little of the marzipan into the general shape of the nose, lips, eyebrows and cheeks. This will sit underneath the main layer of marzipan to give the general features of the face.

Roll out the rest of the marzipan to create a circle large enough to cover the cake with a thickness of 4mm [¼in]. Place on top of the cake and marzipan face features, then trim the edges.

Define the features with a ball modelling tool, creating the eye sockets, nostrils, lips, etc. Eventually it will all be covered in marzipan leaves, but it's important to have the right structure underneath.

Place the jelly eyes below the eyebrow area, then start cutting out some leaf shapes. I used leaf cookie cutters, but I also cut out my own shapes with a knife and scored the leaf veins with the back of the knife.

Create the eyelids with some of the leaf designs, then work your way from the middle of the face outwards using different leaf cutters.

Mould some little mushrooms and acorns out of the remaining marzipan and place them around the face.

Brush some bronze lustre dust on the edges of the leaves and the acorns. Garnish with edible flowers, if you happen to have some. Serve.

S'MORE RAT TARTS

MAKES 10-12

PASTRY
300g [2¼ cups] plain [all-purpose] flour, plus extra for dusting
½ tsp salt
1 tsp icing [confectioners'] sugar
225g [scant 1 cup] unsalted butter, cut into cubes
4–5 Tbsp ice-cold water

FILLING
350ml [1½ cups] double [heavy] cream
280g [1²/₃ cups] chopped good-quality dark chocolate, at least 70% cocoa solids
3 Tbsp caster [granulated] sugar
large pinch of salt
2 large eggs

MERINGUE
2 large egg whites
100g [½ cup] caster [granulated] sugar
pinch of salt
½ tsp vanilla extract

TO DECORATE
100g [3½oz] white modelling chocolate or fondant
25g [1oz] black modelling chocolate or fondant
pink edible powder colouring
black edible powder colouring
black edible ink pen
a little shop-bought royal icing

EQUIPMENT
food processor
8 x 7cm [2¾in] tart rings
electric hand whisk
blowtorch
piping [pastry] bag
small round piping nozzle
ball modelling tool

There was no room left in my last book for these cheeky tarts, but I'm very happy to be able to include them here. These are s'mores on another level - buttery tart base with a decadent salted chocolate custard, topped with torched Swiss meringue. The decorations are so simple to make, and they will go down a treat with guests on Bonfire Night. I've used a fairly small tart ring (7cm/2¾in) to make them individual portions, but feel free to use whatever you have at home.

Put the flour, salt and sugar into a food processor and pulse a couple of times to combine. Add the cubed butter and pulse until the mixture resembles breadcrumbs. Alternatively, do this with your hands. Add the water, 1 Tbsp at a time, until the mixture forms large clumps and holds together when you press it in your hand.

Tip the dough onto a work surface and knead it a couple of times to bring it together. Form into a ball, then flatten it, cover in cling film [plastic wrap] and refrigerate for 10–15 minutes.

Preheat the oven to 180°C fan [400°F/Gas mark 6].

Roll out the pastry on a lightly floured surface until it is 3mm [⅛in] thick, then use to line the 8 tart rings. Don't trim the edges just yet. Line the pastry shells with baking paper and fill with rice or baking beans, then blind bake for 15 minutes. Remove the beans and paper, trim the edges and bake for a further 7–8 minutes. Set the tart shells aside.

Reduce the oven temperature to 160°C fan [350°F/Gas Mark 4].

To make the filling, pour the cream into a small saucepan over a low–medium heat until it reaches simmering point. Do not let it boil. Put the chopped chocolate in a heatproof bowl and pour the hot cream over it. Leave it to stand for a couple of minutes.

cont ...

Fold the chocolate in with a spatula until it is melted and fully combined, then mix in the sugar and a large pinch of salt. Add the eggs and whisk until fully combined.

Pour the filling equally among the tarts and bake for 10–15 minutes until the custard is set. Remove the tarts from the oven, then carefully take them out of the rings and leave to cool on a wire rack.

To make the Swiss meringue, place the egg whites, sugar and salt in a heatproof bowl and mix with a whisk. Place the bowl over a pan of boiling water, making sure the base of the bowl doesn't touch the water, and mix until the egg whites reach a temperature of 70°C [158°F], or you can feel the sugar has dissolved by rubbing the mixture between your fingers.

Take the bowl off the heat and, using an electric hand whisk, beat the mixture on medium speed for 4 minutes. Add the vanilla and continue mixing until you reach stiff peaks that only droop slightly when you lift the whisk. By this point, the bowl should no longer feel hot to the touch. Transfer the meringue to a piping bag. Pipe the meringue on top of the tarts and blowtorch them until lightly coloured.

Using a small round piping nozzle, pipe the whiskers out of royal icing onto a piece of baking paper in a zigzag shape so they look electrified. Leave to dry completely, about 1 hour.

Mould the ears, eyes, nose and tail out of white modelling chocolate or fondant. Add a little black on top of the white bit of the nose and create nostrils with a toothpick or ball modelling tool. Brush a little pink powder colour inside the ears. In the meringue base, create the eye sockets with a ball modelling tool, then insert the eyes. Colour around them with the black powder colour and draw on the pupil with the pen. Drizzle some royal icing in a zigzag over the tail. Repeat to make features for all the tarts.

Place the remaining features on the tarts and serve.

CHRISTMAS BAUBLE
CHOCOLATE SPIDERS

MAKES 12

100g [3½oz] dark chocolate,
at least 70% cocoa solids,
chopped into equal-sized
pieces
piping gel
edible glitter
100g [3½oz] modelling
chocolate (I used dark)
silver edible paint
gold edible paint

EQUIPMENT
24 semi-sphere silicone mould
with 3cm [1¼in] diameter
holes
paintbrushes

Let me tell you the tale of the friendly Christmas
spider. It's a heart-warming Eastern European story
that inspired these chocolate spiders. Legend tells
that a widowed mother had no money to decorate
the Christmas tree for her children, so a friendly
spider came down from the attic to create elaborate
cobwebs all over the pine tree. On Christmas
morning, the mother and her children woke up,
opened the curtains and when the sunlight hit the
spiderwebs, they turned silver and gold - and that's
where the tradition of decorating the tree with tinsel
at Christmas comes from.

Melt the chocolate in a microweavable bowl in the
microwave, working in 20–30-second intervals.

Pour the melted chocolate into the holes of the
semi-sphere mould and spread it around with a brush,
making sure it covers the whole mould. Leave to set
completely, about 30 minutes.

Unmould the chocolate semi-spheres. Stick 2 of them
together by melting them slightly on a hot plate and
then sticking them together to form a ball. Repeat with
the remaining semi-spheres.

Brush some piping gel on each ball and cover in edible
glitter (whichever colours you like).

Mould the little cord attachments at the tops of the
baubles out of modelling chocolate and make a hole
in the centres. Roll the cords out of more modelling
chocolate, bend them into a loop and fix them in place
in the holes you made in the cord attachments.

Make the spider heads out of more modelling
chocolate – mine were 1cm [½ in] – and attach them to
the baubles with a little melted chocolate. To make the
legs, roll them out of modelling chocolate, bend them
and leave them to harden for 10 minutes, then attach
them to the baubles with some melted chocolate.

Paint the cords and attachments at the top with silver
or gold edible paint.

MANDRAKE CAKE

MAKES 2

100g [¾ cup] plain [all-purpose] flour
200g [1 cup] caster [granulated] sugar
3 Tbsp cocoa powder
1 tsp bicarbonate of soda [baking soda]
½ tsp baking powder
½ tsp salt
120ml [½ cup] buttermilk
60ml [¼ cup] vegetable oil
1 large egg
1 tsp vanilla extract
1 tsp instant coffee
120ml [½ cup] hot water

BUTTERCREAM
60g [¼ cup] unsalted butter, softened
¼ tsp salt
½ tsp vanilla extract
300g [2 cups plus 2 Tbsp] icing [confectioners'] sugar, sifted
2 Tbsp cocoa powder
1 Tbsp milk (optional)
½ packet Oreo cookies, roughly crushed

TO DECORATE
A4 sheet rice paper
green food colouring
5ml [1 tsp] vodka
1kg [2¼lb] white modelling chocolate
brown food colouring
red food colouring

EQUIPMENT
2 x 15cm [6in] tall terracotta pots
electric stand mixer
florist's wire
edible glue

To most people, the mandrake root would be recognised from its cameo appearance in the second Harry Potter movie, *Harry Potter and the Chamber of Secrets*. The mandrake, however, has played an important role in the history of witchcraft and shamanism. Much like the fly agaric, the mandrake possesses hallucinogenic and potentially deadly properties. It was often used medicinally as well as recreationally.

Due to its human-like shape, this plant was the subject of legends and myths. It was believed that the mandrake would emit a scream capable of killing if you uprooted it from the ground without covering your ears. Allegedly, these myths were created by witches trying to protect the plant from the masses, as they often used the root and leaves for potions.

In cake form, the mandrake is perfectly safe; in fact, it is rather delicious. I like to use real terracotta pots for these cakes, filled with a rich chocolate sponge, topped with chocolate buttercream and 'edible soil'. The plant is sculpted out of modelling chocolate and the leaves are made from painted rice paper.

Preheat the oven to 180°C fan (400°F/Gas mark 6) and line the base and sides of your terracotta pots with baking paper or non-stick foil.
  Sift the flour, sugar, cocoa powder, bicarbonate of soda, baking powder and salt into a medium bowl and set aside.
  Place the buttermilk, oil, egg and vanilla extract in an electric stand mixer fitted with a paddle attachment and mix on medium speed until fully combined. Reduce the speed to low and slowly add the dry ingredients to the wet until all the ingredients are mixed together.
  Dissolve the instant coffee in the hot water, then add to the cake batter and mix in until combined. Divide the batter equally between the 2 prepared pots, leaving enough space for the buttercream and 'edible soil'.

cont …

Place on a baking tray in the centre of the oven and bake for 35–40 minutes until a skewer inserted into the centre of the cakes comes out clean. Remove from the oven and leave to cool completely in the pots.

While the cakes are cooling, make the buttercream. Mix the butter in an electric mixer until light and fluffy. Add the salt and vanilla, then slowly add the icing sugar and cocoa powder and mix until all the ingredients are incorporated. Check the consistency and add the milk, using more or less as necessary.

Top the cooled sponges with a layer of chocolate buttercream, then sprinkle over some crushed Oreo cookies to imitate the soil.

To make the mandrake leaves, cut leaf shapes out of rice paper, then mix a little of your green food colouring with a few drops of vodka, and paint them green (you could use a silicone veiner to create the veins in the leaves, but this is optional). Leave to dry for 15 minutes.

To mould the mandrakes, start by creating a cone-like shape for the body with a flat base out of the white modelling chocolate. Mark where the eyes and mouth will be and build the shape around those features with extra modelling chocolate, blending with your main body as you go.

Place the mandrake in the middle of your pot and start shaping the arms to go at each side using more modelling chocolate, hanging them over the rim. Create shoots coming out of the arms with the modelling chocolate and blend them in. Add 2 or 3 thicker shoots to go on top of its head. This is where the leaves will be placed. Repeat to make the second mandrake.

Mix some brown colouring with a bit of red and a few drops of vodka to thin it out (or use an airbrush gun if you have one), then paint the mandrakes all over, making the cracks, eyes and mouths darker in colour to create depth.

Once the leaves are fully dried, pinch them at the base and attach them to some florist's wire using edible glue. Stick them in each shoot on the mandrake's head.

SHRUNKEN HEADS GINGERBREAD

MAKES 8-10

450g [3⅓ cups] plain [all-
  purpose] flour
½ tsp baking powder
½ tsp bicarbonate of soda
  [baking soda]
½ tsp salt
1 Tbsp ground ginger
1¾ tsp ground cinnamon
¼ tsp ground cloves
6 Tbsp unsalted butter, at
  room temperature
165g [¾ cup minus 1 Tbsp]
  soft dark brown sugar
1 large egg
230g [⅔ cup] golden [light
  corn] syrup, maple syrup
  or molasses
2 tsp vanilla extract

TO DECORATE
white modelling chocolate
  or fondant
50g [1¾oz] shop-bought
  royal icing
black edible ink pen
edible black lustre dust
brown food colouring

EQUIPMENT
ball modelling tool
piping [pastry] bag

I saw a display of shrunken heads in Oxford
University Museum of Natural History a couple
of years ago. I took some photos and have been
planning to make them into cookies ever since. The
tradition of shrinking heads originates in northern
Peru and eastern Ecuador, home to the Jivaroan
peoples. They believed that by shrinking the head of
an opponent, you would harness the spirit of your
enemy and he would serve you for eternity, although
they were also used as battle trophies. The process
is rather gruesome, so I won't describe it here, right
before you make your edible version.

Sift the flour, baking powder, bicarbonate of soda,
salt and spices into a large bowl and set aside.
  In another bowl, mix the butter, brown sugar and
egg together. I like to use a wooden spoon for this.
Somehow gingerbread seems like it has to be mixed
with a wooden spoon. Add the syrup and vanilla
and continue to mix. Mix in the dry ingredients and
combine until smooth.
  Divide the dough in half and wrap in clingfilm
[plastic wrap] pressing down to create 2 discs.
Refrigerate for 3 hours, or up to 3 days.
  Preheat the oven to 190°C fan [410°F/Gas Mark 6½]
and line 2 baking trays with silicone mats or sheets of
baking paper.
  Take a piece of dough and mould it into a skull shape
in your hands, wider at the top. My skulls were 7cm
[2¾ in] high. Using a ball modelling tool, make the eye
socket incisions. Pinch the nose and create the nostrils
with the ball modelling tool.

cont …

Add more dough to the cheeks and the eyebrows and blend into the face. Create the mouth and some wrinkles. Repeat with the rest of the dough until it's all used up. Each head will be different, which is exactly what you want.

Place in the freezer for 10 minutes, then bake for 10–12 minutes until the edges start browning. Remove from the oven and leave to cool.

Create the eyeballs with modelling chocolate or fondant and stick in the eye sockets with a little royal icing. Draw the irises with the pen. Brush around the eyes with the black powder colour and finally, pipe the threads around the mouth with brown royal icing. Store for up to a month.

'GHOST OF CHRISTMAS PAST' COOKIES

MAKES ABOUT 24,
DEPENDING ON THE SIZE
OF YOUR GHOST

300g [2½ cups] plain [all-
purpose] flour, plus extra for
dusting
½ tsp bicarbonate of soda
[baking soda]
½ tsp cream of tartar
¼ tsp salt
225g [1 cup] unsalted butter,
at room temperature
185g [¾ cup plus 2 Tbsp]
caster [granulated] sugar
1 large egg
1 tsp vanilla extract
½ tsp almond extract
black food paint
400g [14oz] tub shop-bought
royal icing
250g [9oz] packet modelling
chocolate or fondant in red,
green, yellow and blue

EQUIPMENT
electric stand mixer
paintbrush
piping [pastry] bag

These adorable little spirits are coming out to help
you decorate the tree on Christmas Eve. I can't get
enough of spooky Christmas bakes, and these are
such a fun project to bake with the family. If you have
a ghost cookie cutter, great! But it's a simple shape to
draw on a piece of card and use as a template, if not.

Sift the flour, bicarbonate of soda, cream of tartar and
salt into a medium-sized bowl. Set aside.

Place the butter and sugar in an electric stand mixer
fitted with a paddle attachment and cream until light
and fluffy. Add the egg and extracts and continue
mixing until fully combined.

Add the flour mixture and mix until the dough
comes together. Wrap in clingfilm [plastic wrap] and
refrigerate for at least 2 hours.

When you're ready to start baking, preheat the oven
to 180°C fan [400°F/Gas mark 6] and line 2 baking
sheets with silicone mats or baking paper.

Roll out the dough on a lightly floured surface until it
is 4mm [¼in] thick and cut out the ghost shapes. Place
on the prepared baking trays and bake for 7–8 minutes.

As soon as they are out of the oven, place a piece
of baking paper on top of each cookie and smooth
the surface with a small baking tray, making circular
movements on top of each cookie. Transfer to a wire
rack and leave to cool completely – about 30 minutes.

To decorate, paint the eyes and mouth area on each
cookie black with some edible paint, then using royal
icing, cover the entire ghost except the eyes and mouth.
Leave to dry completely.

To make the lights, I used a silicone fairy light
mould using different coloured modelling chocolate or
fondant. You can mould them by hand, but it's easier
with a mould. They are available online. Paint the metal
bit of each light bulb gold.

Colour some royal icing black. Pipe the electric cables
onto each cookie with the black coloured royal icing,
then attach the little light bulbs using some more royal
icing. Store for up to 2 weeks.

CHOCOLATE PEANUT BUTTER FLIES

MAKES 10

130g [½ cup] smooth peanut
  butter
3 Tbsp icing [confectioners']
  sugar, sifted
150g [5¼oz] milk or dark
  chocolate, chopped
50g [1¾oz] red modelling
  chocolate or fondant
100g [3½oz] clear isomalt
2 squares white chocolate,
  to use as glue for the wings

EQUIPMENT
silicone veiner

I'm sure I declared my obsession with peanut butter cups in my previous book. Turning the chocolate peanut butter combination into different creatures might just become something I do every year, like putting my Halloween decorations out. Use a silicone veiner to create the wings, or just pour them onto baking paper.

In a small bowl, mix the peanut butter with the icing sugar until fully incorporated. Refrigerate for 15 minutes.

Line a baking tray with baking paper. Take the peanut butter mixture out of the fridge and shape into 10 ovals (for the bodies) and 10 balls (for the heads). Stick together to create 10 flies, then place on the lined baking tray and chill for another 15 minutes.

Melt the milk or dark chocolate in a microweavable bowl in the microwave, working in 30-second intervals.

Remove the peanut butter bodies from the fridge and dip them into the melted chocolate, then place back on the baking paper.

Make the eyes out of the red modelling chocolate or fondant and stick them on with a little of the melted chocolate.

To make the wings, melt the isomalt according to the packet instructions and, using a teaspoon, pour into a wing shape on a silicone veiner or baking paper. Leave to cool.

Meanwhile, melt the white chocolate in a microwaveable bowl in the microwave, working in 20–30-second intervals.

Once the wings are cool, attach them to the body with a little melted white chocolate. Pipe the legs onto baking paper using the leftover milk or dark chocolate and leave to set, then attach them to the body with a little more melted chocolate. They're fiddly, so be patient.

VIENNESE SNAKES ∽

MAKES 8-10

100g [7 Tbsp] unsalted butter,
  softened
2½ Tbsp icing [confectioners']
  sugar
½ tsp vanilla extract
1 Tbsp milk
110g [1 cup minus 2 tsp]
  plain [all-purpose] flour
1 Tbsp matcha powder
¼ tsp baking powder
pinch of salt
100g [3½oz] white chocolate,
  chopped
handful of green Candy Melts
50g [⅓ cup] shelled
  pistachios, chopped
yellow cocoa-based food
  colouring
red cocoa-based food
  colouring

EQUIPMENT
electric stand mixer
piping [pastry] bag fitted with
  a round nozzle
piping [pastry] bag fitted with
  a large star nozzle
black edible ink pen

I know that matcha isn't everyone's cup of tea. In all honesty, it isn't mine either. That is, until you pair it with white chocolate and some nuts. The combination is ideal. A matcha made in hell. However, if you feel you would rather not have it, substitute the matcha powder for cornflour [cornstarch] and add some green food colouring.

Preheat the oven to 160°C fan [350°F/Gas mark 4] and line a baking sheet with a silicone mat or baking paper.

Cream the butter and icing sugar together in an electric stand mixer fitted with a paddle attachment for 3–4 minutes until light and fluffy. Add the vanilla extract and milk and continue mixing.

Sift the flour, matcha powder, baking powder and salt into a large bowl, then fold into the butter-and-sugar mixture with a spatula until you get a tacky dough.

Pour a quarter of the batter into a piping [pastry] bag fitted with a round nozzle and the rest into a piping bag fitted with a large star nozzle.

Pipe the heads of the snakes onto the lined baking sheet with the round nozzle, then pipe swirling shapes for the bodies using the star nozzle bag. You should be able to make 8–10 snakes. Bake for 10–12 minutes. Remove from the oven and leave to cool completely on a wire rack.

Melt the white chocolate (reserving enough for the eyes and tongue) with a few green Candy Melts to give it a green tint in a microwaveable bowl in the microwave, working in 20–30-second intervals.

Dip the snakes diagonally into the green melted chocolate and sprinkle with the nuts.

Melt the reserved white chocolate and colour half of it yellow and half red. Pipe the yellow eyes and red tongue onto the snakes and leave to cool. Once cooled, draw a line in black in the middle of the eyes. Store for 3–4 days.

BRIDE OF FRANKENSTEIN CUPCAKES

115g [1 cup minus 1 tsp]
  plain [all-purpose] flour
2 Tbsp cocoa powder
¼ tsp bicarbonate of soda
  [baking soda]
¼ tsp salt
60g [¼ cup] unsalted butter,
  softened
140g [¾ cup minus 2 tsp]
  caster [granulated] sugar
1 large egg
1 tsp vanilla extract
80ml [⅓ cup] buttermilk
1 tsp instant coffee, dissolved
  in 3 Tbsp hot water

BUTTERCREAM
60g [¼ cup] unsalted butter,
  softened
¼ tsp salt
½ tsp vanilla extract
300g [2 cups plus 2 Tbsp]
  icing [confectioners'] sugar,
  sifted
1 Tbsp milk
2 Tbsp cocoa powder
black gel food colouring

TO DECORATE
½ tsp cocoa powder
black gel food colouring
100g [3½oz] green modelling
  chocolate or fondant
black edible ink pen
edible blood
50g [1¾oz] shop-bought royal
  icing, coloured black
edible red lustre dust
12 ice-cream cones (optional)

EQUIPMENT
12-hole muffin tin
12 gold cupcake cases
electric stand mixer
piping [pastry] bag fitted with
  large star nozzle
smaller round nozzle

What a treat for those who love the frosting more than the sponge. (That's not me by the way: I love a good sponge.) The cupcakes need to have a chocolate frosting in order to get the black colour, so I've opted for a chocolate sponge, but you could use vanilla or any other cupcake that would complement the chocolate.

Preheat the oven to 180°C fan [400°F/Gas mark 6] and line a 12-hole muffin tin with cupcake cases.

Sift the flour, cocoa, bicarbonate of soda and salt into a medium bowl and set aside.

Cream the butter and sugar together in an electric stand mixer fitted with a paddle attachment on medium speed until light and fluffy. Add the egg and vanilla extract and continue mixing. Reduce the speed to low and add the dry ingredients, alternating with the buttermilk. Add the dissolved coffee and continue mixing until fully combined.

Divide the batter between the paper cases and bake for 14–16 minutes until a toothpick inserted in the middle comes out clean. Leave to cool completely on a wire rack before decorating.

To make the buttercream, mix the butter on its own in an electric stand mixer until light and fluffy. Add the salt and vanilla extract, then slowly add the icing sugar. Check the consistency and add more or less milk if necessary. Set aside 3–4 Tbsp of this uncoloured buttercream for the white hair strips, then add the cocoa powder and black food colouring to the rest and continue mixing until fully combined.

To decorate the cupcakes, roll out the modelling chocolate or fondant until it is 3mm [⅛in] thick. Cut out a circle slightly bigger than the diameter of the cupcake top. Spread a thin layer of frosting on the cupcake and top with the fondant.

cont ...

Paint the closed eyes and eyelashes using your edible ink pen. Cut open a little scar or two in the fondant or modelling chocolate and fill it with edible blood, then prick the holes for the stitches and pipe the thread with black coloured royal icing. Dust some red powder on the cheeks.

To pipe the buttercream hair, fill a piping bag fitted with a large star nozzle with the black buttercream and pipe as high as you can. Do the same with a smaller round nozzle for the white hair and pipe a zigzag line on the side.

If you struggle to get the hair very tall, you can just use an ice-cream cone and pipe around it.

COFFIN MINCE PIE

MAKES 2 PIES (SERVES 4)

PASTRY
500g [3¾ cups] plain [all-purpose] flour
1½ tsp table salt
55g [¼ cup minus 1 tsp] unsalted butter
55g [¼ cup minus 1 tsp] lard [shortening]
280ml [1 cup plus 2 Tbsp] water
1 egg yolk, beaten, for brushing

FILLING
1 Tbsp olive oil
1 yellow onion, finely chopped
2 garlic cloves, minced
500g [2¼ cups] minced [ground] beef
2 tsp ground cumin
½ tsp chilli powder
salt and pepper
1 Tbsp cornflour [cornstarch]
100g [¾ cup] sultanas [golden raisins]
splash of red wine
240ml [1 cup] beef stock

EQUIPMENT
printer
cardboard
masking tape
kitchen scissors

Having learned that the original mince pies were encased in pastry shells called coffins (see page 10), I must include them as a recipe in this book. As I mentioned before, the original mince pie was a meat pie, larger than the sweet individual ones we eat at Christmas. It also contained raisins or sultanas [golden raisins], making the origins of this very British sweet treat a bit more familiar. To create the coffin shape, I made a cardboard coffin-shaped box without a lid, 18cm [7in] long, 8cm [3¼in] at the widest point and 5cm [2in] high, then covered it in foil. I've used hot water crust pastry here, as it's similar to the original pastry used in the 1500s.

Print out a coffin-shaped box template (there's loads to choose from online). Make it out of cardboard using masking tape to stick it together, then cover it in foil.

Sift the flour and salt into a large bowl and set aside.

Bring the butter, lard and water to the boil in a saucepan. Make a well in the centre of your flour mixture and add the water and fat to it. Mix with a wooden spoon until you get a dough. Knead the dough a couple of times to bring it together, then flatten into a disc and cover in clingfilm [plastic wrap]. Refrigerate while you make your filling.

Preheat the oven to 180°C fan [400°F/Gas mark 6].

Heat the oil in a large frying pan [skillet] over a low–medium heat and fry the onion and garlic for about 5 minutes, or until softened. Add the meat and continue cooking for another 5–6 minutes until browned. Sprinkle in the cumin, chilli powder and salt and pepper. Stir in the cornflour, then add the sultanas. Continue cooking for 2 minutes. Add the red wine and stock and cook for 5 minutes, or until the stock reduces and thickens. Remove from the heat and leave to cool.

cont …

Remove the pastry from the fridge and divide into 2 equal-sized pieces. Set aside about a third of each half for the pie lids. Roll out one of the larger pieces of pastry until it's 3mm [1/8mm] thick and use it to line the inside of one of your foil-covered coffin boxes. Repeat with the other large piece of pastry. Fill the coffins with the meat filling. Roll out the 2 smaller pieces of pastry to a thickness of 3mm [1/8mm] thick and place on top of the coffins as lids, sealing them shut with your fingers. Trim the edges with scissors and crimp.

If you are serving the pies during Yule, use some of the leftover pastry to make some holly leaves and berries. Brush the top with the beaten egg yolk and cut a cross to allow the steam to escape. Bake for 35–40 minutes until golden brown. Serve immediately.

DEMONSHIRE SPLIT ～

MAKES 12

500g [3½ cups] strong white
bread flour, plus extra for
dusting
2 Tbsp caster [granulated]
sugar
1 tsp salt
2 tsp instant dried yeast
2 Tbsp unsalted butter, melted
300ml [1¼ cups] warm milk
cooking oil, for oiling

FILLING
blanched whole almonds
clotted or whipped cream
white chocolate, melted (to
attach the teeth)
200g [7oz] pink modelling
chocolate or fondant
edible red lustre dust
piping gel
strawberry or raspberry jam

EQUIPMENT
electric stand mixer
piping [pastry] bag

A Devonshire split is a soft enriched bread roll filled
with clotted cream and jam. It gets split rather than
cut open, hence its name. As soon as I saw one, I
immediately thought of a gruesome open mouth with
sharp teeth and 'blood' jam oozing from it. These
buns date back to the 10th century, but they're still
worth making and eating ... before they eat you!

Place the flour in an electric stand mixer fitted with a
dough hook attachment. Add the sugar and salt to one
side and the yeast to the other. Pour in the butter and
most of the milk (you may not need it all) and turn the
machine on. Knead the dough for 5 minutes, adding
the rest of the milk if necessary. When the dough looks
smooth and elastic, place it in an oiled bowl, cover with
a damp tea towel and leave to rise in a warm place for
1 hour, or until it has doubled in size.

Line 2 baking trays with silicone mats or sheets of
baking paper.

Tip the dough out onto a lightly floured surface and
knead it a couple of times to knock out the air. Divide
into 12 equal-sized pieces and roll each one into a ball.

Place the balls well apart from each other on the lined
baking trays, cover with oiled clingfilm [plastic wrap]
and leave to prove in a warm place for 30 minutes.

Preheat the oven to 200°C fan [425°F/Gas mark 7].

Bake for 10–15 minutes until golden and well risen.
Remove from the oven and leave to cool on a wire rack.

Carve the almonds into sharp teeth using a small,
sharp knife. Cut a slit in the buns, fill with the cream
and attach the teeth (with melted white chocolate if
necessary) to the top and bottom, leaving space at the
bottom for the tongue.

Make the tongues by shaping the pink modelling
chocolate or fondant – it helps to look at a picture of a
tongue. Mark a line in the middle and prick little holes
all around for the taste buds. Add red lustre dust to the
sides and middle, then piping gel to make it look wet.
Place the tongues inside the buns and pipe the 'blood'
jam around the teeth and inside the demonshire split.

CRACKED BROWNIE COOKIES

MAKES 22-24

225g [8oz] dark chocolate,
  at least 70% cocoa solids,
  chopped
65g [¼ cup plus 1 tsp]
  unsalted butter, cubed
95g [¾ cup] plain [all-
  purpose] flour
1½ Tbsp cocoa powder
½ tsp baking powder
¼ tsp salt
2 large eggs
150g [¾ cup] caster
  [granulated] sugar
50g [¼ cup] brown sugar
1 tsp vanilla extract
large handful of chopped
  shelled pistachios
sea salt, for sprinkling
edible red lustre dust
edible black lustre dust
50g [1¾oz] shop-bought
  royal icing

EQUIPMENT
ball modelling tool
piping [pastry] bag

A cross between a cookie and a brownie, but with a chilling touch. It's a fairly simple touch mind you, but effective. Not giving the cookies any other facial features apart from the mouth makes them even more creepy, which is always welcome.

Preheat the oven to 180°C fan [400°F/Gas mark 6] and line 2 baking trays with silicone mats or baking paper.

Melt the dark chocolate and butter in a microweavable bowl in the microwave, working in 30-second intervals. Alternatively, melt the chocolate and butter in a heatproof bowl set over a pan of gently simmering water, making sure the base of the bowl doesn't touch the water. Set aside.

In a medium-sized bowl, sift the flour, cocoa powder, baking powder and salt together.

In a separate bowl and using an electric whisk, mix the eggs, sugars and vanilla together until fully combined. Add the melted chocolate mixture and keep mixing. Add the flour mixture and continue mixing until fully combined.

Drop 1 heaped Tbsp dough per cookie on the prepared trays, spacing them well apart as they will spread during baking. Sprinkle with chopped pistachios, leaving the mouth area free of nuts, and bake for 12–14 minutes until glossy and crackled.

Remove from the oven and sprinkle with salt. Leave to cool for a few minutes, but while the cookies are still warm, make an indentation for the mouth in each one, using a ball modelling tool. Leave to cool completely.

Once cooled, paint the interior of the mouths with the lustre dust in either red or black, and pipe the teeth with royal icing. Store for up to 3 days.

THE TIPSY WITCH

GIGGLEWATER

SERVES 2

2 Tbsp fresh lemon juice
2 tsp syrup from the candied
 lemons (see below)
75ml [2½fl oz] gin
crushed ice
champagne, for topping up

CANDIED LEMONS
1 lemon
225ml [scant 1 cup] water
200g [1 cup] granulated sugar

EQUIPMENT
cocktail shaker
2 champagne glasses

The idea for gigglewater comes from the adorable art deco underground club seen in the film *Fantastic Beasts and Where to Find Them*. However, the term actually exists. It's an American slang word used to refer to an alcoholic beverage during the Prohibition era. It was particularly used to refer to champagne, which is the dominant ingredient in this recipe.

Make the candied lemons first. Cut the lemon into slices, about 5mm [¼in] thick, then remove and discard the pips.

Heat the water and sugar in a large saucepan over a low heat, stirring, until the sugar is completely dissolved. Add the lemon slices and cook for about 30 minutes, or until they become translucent. Remove the slices from the pan (reserving 2 tsp of the syrup), and leave to dry out on a silicone mat or some baking paper for 12 hours.

To make the cocktail, combine the lemon juice, the candied lemon syrup and the gin in a cocktail shaker and fill it up with crushed ice. Shake well and strain into 2 champagne glasses. Top up with champagne, stir and garnish with a slice of candied lemon.

LAVENDER LEMONADE

MAKES 1.5 LITRES [6¼ CUPS]

500ml [2 cups] water
200g [1 cup] granulated sugar
3 Tbsp dried lavender buds
750ml [3¼ cups] ice-cold
   water
juice of 8–10 lemons
purple food colouring
   (optional)

EQUIPMENT
muslin cloth [cheesecloth]
large jar

The combination of lemon and lavender is a true summer witch treat. I spoke of the medicinal properties of lavender in the apothecary section (page 72); however, lavender also serves an excellent culinary ally. Lavender belongs to the same family as rosemary, therefore it can be used in an identical way: for meat rubs, infusions or in baking. Lavender is the first herb I ever planted, and I harvest and use it all year around.

Start by making the lavender syrup. Combine the water and sugar in a saucepan over a medium heat and stir until the sugar is fully dissolved. Bring to the boil, then remove from the heat and add the lavender buds. Allow the mixture to infuse for a couple of hours, then strain the syrup through a muslin cloth [cheesecloth] into a bowl, squeezing out all the juices.
   In a large jug [pitcher], combine the lavender syrup, ice-cold water and lemon juice. Taste and adjust the sugar and/or lemon juice. I like it quite tart. Add a couple of drops of purple food colouring if you like a more vibrant hue, then serve.

MELTING GHOST COCKTAIL ⌒⌒

SERVES 2

INGREDIENTS
85ml [2¾fl oz] coffee liqueur
85ml [2¾fl oz] chocolate
    liqueur
60ml [4 Tbsp] single [light]
    cream
crushed ice
freshly grated nutmeg
white candy floss
black edible paint

EQUIPMENT
cocktail shaker
2 small flute glasses
small paintbrush

This is such a fun and tasty cocktail to make for a night of frivolity in the company of your favourite ghouls. Make sure to use small fluted glasses for this cocktail, as the candy floss ghost will need to sit above the drink to avoid it melting before it hits your tongue.

Pour the coffee and chocolate liqueurs and cream into a cocktail shaker and add some crushed ice. Shake until chilled and combined, then strain into 2 small flute glasses. Grate some nutmeg on top to garnish.
  Roll the candy floss into a ghostly shape and paint the eyes with black edible paint. Place on the top of each glass, making sure they don't touch the drink.
  Melt into the drink before consuming.

WHITE WITCH ~ↄ

SERVES 1

25ml [1fl oz] vodka
25ml [1fl oz] Kahlúa
50ml [1¾fl oz] Baileys Irish
  Cream liqueur
60ml [¼ cup] milk
crushed ice

WITCH HAT
50g [1¾oz] white chocolate,
  chopped into small pieces
1 plain Bugles crisp [cone-
  shaped corn snacks]
1 Oreo cookie, halved
desiccated [dry unsweetened]
  coconut, for sprinkling

EQUIPMENT
brush
cocktail shaker
1 glass

It seems it's going to become a tradition for GBBO Michael Chakraverty to sneak a recipe into every book I write. That's absolutely fine with me. This drink is the witchy cousin of the white Russian. To finish it off, I have made a white chocolate witch hat.

To make the witch hat, melt the chocolate in a microwaveable bowl in the microwave, working in 30-second intervals. Alternatively, put the chocolate into a heatproof bowl set over a pan of gently simmering water, making sure the base of the bowl doesn't touch the water, and leave until melted. Dip the base of the Bugle into the melted chocolate and attach to one half of the Oreo cookie (eat the other half!). Using a brush, paint the hat shape with the melted chocolate and sprinkle with the coconut. Set aside on baking paper.
  Combine the vodka, Kahlúa, Baileys, milk and crushed ice in a cocktail shaker. Shake well and strain into a glass. Top with the witch hat and serve.

MAD WITCH POTION

SERVES 2

90ml [3fl oz] vodka
45ml [1½fl oz] blue Curaçao
180ml [¾ cup] pineapple juice
180ml [¾ cup] orange juice
crushed ice

EQUIPMENT
cocktail shaker
dry ice
2 potion bottles
tongs

The colour of this cocktail is truly mesmerizing. I thought it would be fun to serve it in the little potion bottles that I actually stock in my shop. To add to the look, you can buy dry ice online: just make sure you handle it carefully, and that it is fully melted before you take a sip.

Put the vodka, blue Curaçao, pineapple juice and orange juice into a cocktail shaker. Top with crushed ice and shake until cooled.

Pour into 2 potion bottles and drop a little piece of dry ice into each one using tongs. Leave until the dry ice has completely melted before drinking.

BUBBLE BUBBLE TEA
(WITH TAPIOCA FROG SPAWN)

SERVES 2

TAPIOCA FROG SPAWN
2 Tbsp boiling water
6 Tbsp tapioca flour
500ml [2 cups] water

TEA
2 tsp matcha tea powder
4 Tbsp hot water
4 Tbsp maple syrup
480ml [2 cups minus 4 tsp]
    oat milk
handful of ice cubes
Tapioca Frog Spawn (see
    above) or 100g [½ cup]
    pre-cooked tapioca pearls

EQUIPMENT
blender or food processor
2 tall glasses
bubble tea straws

Bubble bubble, toil and trouble - hold on, it's double double. Never mind. This recipe is a witchy take on the very trendy bubble tea. You can actually buy tapioca pearls that are ready to boil, but I want to give you the option of making your own. Bubble tea can be made in a variety of ways and flavours, but in order to add to the swamp aesthetic, we are making this one green with matcha.

To make the tapioca frog spawn, mix 2 Tbsp boiling water and the tapioca flour together in a small bowl with a fork until it forms a dough you can pick up with your hands. Transfer to a clean surface and knead the dough until it is smooth. Divide the dough into 2 equal pieces and roll them into thin strips. Cut the strips into 5mm [¼in] pieces and roll them into balls in the palm of your hand.
 Bring the 500ml [2 cups] water to the boil in a medium saucepan. Add the tapioca balls and cook for 5 minutes or so. You are looking for a soft and chewy consistency.
 Remove from the heat and leave to rest for a few minutes, then transfer the 'spawn' to a bowl of water to prevent them from sticking together.
 To make the tea, combine the matcha powder and hot water in a small container and let it brew for a couple of minutes.
 Put the maple syrup, oat milk, matcha mixture and the ice into a blender or food processor and blend for a few seconds until all the ingredients are combined.
 Divide the tapioca frog spawn or pre-cooked tapioca pearls between 2 tall glasses and top up with the tea. Add bubble tea straws and enjoy.

BLACK CAT MILKSHAKE ～

SERVES 1

black fondant or dark
  modelling chocolate
orange fondant or modelling
  chocolate
2 scoops chocolate ice cream
250ml [1 cup] milk
1 Tbsp caster [superfine]
  sugar
1½ Tbsp cocoa powder
½ tsp activated charcoal
  powder
120ml [½ cup] double
  [heavy] cream
black gel food colouring

EQUIPMENT
blender
1 glass
handheld electric mixer
piping [pastry] bag fitted
  with a star nozzle

This drink is inspired by those vintage Halloween
scaredy cats you see in old greeting cards. This is
perfect for Halloween morning, just to get you in
the spirit!

Start by making the cat face features out of fondant or
modelling chocolate. Make the ears in black with an
orange interior, then make the eyes, nose and whiskers.
Set aside.

Put the ice cream and milk into a blender and whizz
until fully combined. Pour into your glass.

To make the whipped cream, mix the caster sugar,
cocoa powder and charcoal together in a medium-sized
bowl. Set aside.

Using a handheld electric mixer, whip the double
cream to soft peaks, then start adding the sugar
mixture. Add enough black gel food colouring to
achieve a darker black.

Pour the black whipped cream into a piping bag fitted
with a star nozzle and pipe on top of the shake. Stick
on the cat's ears, eyes, nose and whiskers, then serve
with a straw and spoon.

CHOCOLATE CALIENTE ⌔

SERVES 2

600ml [2½ cups] whole milk
or dairy-free milk
70g [2½oz] dark chocolate,
at least 70% cocoa solids,
chopped
1¼ tsp ground cinnamon
½ vanilla pod [bean], split in
half lengthways and seeds
scraped out
pinch of salt
1 small red chilli, halved and
deseeded
about 1 tsp soft dark brown
sugar

TUILE BAT WINGS
50g [6 Tbsp] plain [all-
purpose] flour
50g [⅓ cup] icing
[confectioners'] sugar
1 extra-large egg white
1 heaped Tbsp cocoa powder
black gel food colouring

EQUIPMENT
electric whisk
piping [pastry] bag

A spicy hot chocolate drink for *brujitas locas* (little mischievous witches). I know you probably wouldn't think of giving chilli chocolate to kids, but my 2-year-old loves a bit of spice, and you can choose the amount of chilli you'd like to add. If making it for older *brujas*, add a shot of brandy to each cup.

Bring the milk to a gentle simmer in a small saucepan over a medium-low heat and whisk in the chocolate until melted. Add the cinnamon, vanilla pod and seeds, salt and chilli. Simmer for a couple of minutes (the longer you simmer, the spicier it will be), then remove from the heat and leave to cool slightly.

Remove and discard the chilli and vanilla pod and mix in the sugar. Taste and adjust to your liking. Set aside.

To make the tuile bat wings, start by drawing a bat wing template onto a piece of paper. My bat wings were 6cm [2½in]. You will need 4 bat wings in total. Line a baking tray with baking paper and place your bat wing template underneath.

Preheat the oven to 180°C fan [400°F/Gas mark 6].

Using an electric whisk, mix the flour, sugar and egg white together, then add the cocoa powder and continue mixing until fully combined. Add black gel food colouring little by little, mixing well until the mixture turns black.

Pour the batter into a piping bag and pipe 2 bat wings thinly, following the template. Now flip the template over under the baking paper and pipe the opposite 2 wings.

Bake for 6–7 minutes. Remove from the oven and place the wings over a rolling pin to curve them. Cut out a little slit at the bottom while they are still hot. This will allow you to place them on the rim of your mug.

Reheat the chocolate gently, then pour into 2 mugs and place 2 bat wings on each rim to serve.

LAMBSWOOL ⌁

MAKES 2 LITRES

1 litre [4 cups] dry cider
1 litre [4 cups] apple juice
6 whole cloves
4 cinnamon sticks, plus extra
  to serve
3 star anise
3cm [1¼in] piece of fresh
  ginger, peeled and cut into
  4 pieces
lemon peel
a few crab apples
brown sugar, to taste
freshly grated nutmeg
shrunken head apples, to
  serve (see intro)

EQUIPMENT
large pot or cauldron

Lambswool or wassail is an old English spiced hot cider drink often associated with Yuletide celebrations. The 'wool' is created when the crab apples burst in the hot cider and create a wool-like top. Crab apples are abundant in early autumn – you see them in car parks as well as city parks – so it shouldn't be too hard to find them. To add an extra witchy touch, carve some of the apples into shrunken heads and serve in a cauldron.

Put the cider, apple juice, cloves, cinnamon sticks, star anise, ginger, lemon peel and crab apples into a large pot or cauldron over a low–medium heat. This could also be heated outside on burning coals. Bring to a gentle simmer, then remove from the heat and taste. Add brown sugar, 1 tsp at a time, if you like it a bit sweeter.

  Serve hot, with shrunken head apples and a cinnamon stick.

WHITE HOT CHOCOLATE
GHOST BOMBS ⌒∿

SERVES 2

40g [¼ cup] white chocolate
  chips or chopped white
  chocolate
¼ tube marshmallow fluff
490ml (2 cups minus 2
  teaspoons) whole milk

EQUIPMENT
ghost ice-cube tray
brush (optional)
piping [pastry] bag
2 cups

Last Christmas, the internet was inundated with videos on how to make hot chocolate bombs: basically, a chocolate sphere filled with marshmallows and maybe other flavours. I thought I would do my own version - white chocolate ghosts filled with marshmallow fluff that melt in hot milk. The mould I used is for ice cubes and it works fine for this recipe. It's available in lots of online shops. I've used it to make bath melts and all sorts, but never for making ice.

Melt the chocolate in a microwaveable bowl in the microwave, working in 30-second intervals. Alternatively, put the chocolate into a heatproof bowl set over a pan of gently simmering water, making sure the base of the bowl doesn't touch the water, and leave until melted.

Pour the melted chocolate into 2 of your ghost moulds, making sure the chocolate covers the entire ghost. You may need to use a brush for this or turn it upside down. Leave to cool and set.

When fully set, fill a piping [pastry] bag with the marshmallow fluff (as it's very sticky), then use to fill the chocolate-lined ghosts. Finish with a layer of chocolate and leave to set completely.

Heat the milk in a pan until warm, then divide the milk into 2 cups and drop a ghost into each. Sit by the fire and enjoy.

INDEX

Publishing Director: Sarah Lavelle
Senior Commissioning Editor: Céline Hughes
Art Direction and Design: Nikki Ellis
Photographer: Patricia Niven
Illustrator: Andrea Kett
Food Stylists: Helena Garcia, Jo Jackson
Prop Stylist: Agathe Gits
Head of Production: Stephen Lang
Production Controller: Sabeena Atchia

Published in 2021 by Quadrille,
an imprint of Hardie Grant Publishing

Quadrille
52–54 Southwark Street
London SE1 1UN
quadrille.com

Cataloguing in Publication Data: a catalogue
record for this book is available from the
British Library.

Text © Helena Garcia 2021
Design and layout © Quadrille 2021
Photography © Patricia Niven 2021

ISBN 978 1 78713 783 7

Printed in China

Acknowledgments

A huge thank you my agent Vivienne for
making this book possible.
   To Céline Hughes for still trusting that
my crazy ideas have a market and to Nikki
Ellis for holding me back when I needed it.
   To Patricia Nivens for always creating the
most beautiful photographs, wonderfully
styled by Agathe Gits.
   To Jo Jackson for help in the kitchen.
   A very special thanks to my darling
Andrea Kett – I wouldn't have had anyone
else illustrate this book.
   And to Caroline Rose, not only for letting
us play in The Cabinet of Curiosities
for a day, but for first introducing me to
the wonder of antique shop fittings. You
created an addict!